Law in the American West

SERIES EDITOR
John R. Wunder,
University of Nebraska-Lincoln

IN COLD STORAGE

Sex and Murder on the Plains

JAMES W. HEWITT

University of Nebraska Press
Lincoln and London

Library of Congress
Cataloging-in-Publication Data
Hewitt, James W.
In cold storage: sex and murder on
the Plains / James W. Hewitt.
pages   cm. — (Law in the American West)
ISBN 978-0-8032-5663-7 (pbk.: alk. paper)
ISBN 978-0-8032-8073-1 (epub)
ISBN 978-0-8032-8074-8 (mobi)
ISBN 978-0-8032-8075-5 (pdf)
1. Murder—Nebraska—McCook—Case
studies. 2. Murder investigation—
Nebraska—McCook—Case
studies. I. Title.
HV6534.M385H49 2015
364.152'309782843—dc23
2014041595

Set in Lyon by M. Scheer.
Designed by N. Putens.

CONTENTS

ILLUSTRATIONS

Following page 58

PREFACE

In 1973, McCook, Nebraska, was like many other rural towns. People lived, worked, and socialized in a generally well-established routine, with infrequent disruptions. Though the people of McCook followed the daily news bulletins of the Watergate scandals, most were more interested in the high school sports team and the local farm news. There were few exceptional events in the small town.

The first signs of fall began to appear in southwestern Nebraska in September that year, as another school year was underway and there was finally some relief from the unusually warm summer. The McCook High Bisons won their first football games of the season, though no one dared dream of another 1960, when the Bisons went undefeated. Life went on as usual. October 1973, however, ushered in a season of fear and suspicion, when the town was shaken by the discovery of the murders of Edwin and Wilma Hoyt.

The Hoyts vanished from their farm home near McCook in September. They remained missing for several days, until gruesome sections of their dismembered bodies floated to the surface of an area lake. Law enforcement personnel and a private investigator worked on the case for months before finally charging McCook resident Harold Nokes and his wife, Ena, with murder. The brilliant and dogged young sheriff who was Harold Nokes's jailor elicited a confession from him. Nokes pleaded guilty; his wife was never convicted of murder, based on Harold's insistence that she had no active role in the deaths. Harold was sentenced to two life sentences in the state penitentiary, where he remains some forty years later. He will never be released. The true story of why and how Harold Nokes murdered Mr. and Mrs. Hoyt remains a mystery. What he said then and what he says now regarding his actions and motive are totally different.

In 1999 I was chair of the Nebraska State Bar Association's Centennial Committee. I wanted to write an article about the Hoyt murders, a well-known and sensational case, for one of the association's publications. The court that had sentenced Harold Nokes, however, had sealed all the court records, because the files were replete with the identities of several McCook citizens who had engaged in tawdry sexual practices with one of the daughters of the Hoyts. The order sealing the files kept me from writing the article. But I decided to investigate the case further.

The prosecutor in the case, who had been a good friend since law school, turned over his personal file to me. I read it all. I learned what Harold Nokes had said during his confession in January of 1974, how and why he claimed he killed the victims, and how he disposed of the bodies.

To learn more about the case, I wanted to speak with Harold Nokes himself. After more than a year of trying to make contact with him, Nokes finally agreed to talk to me. He has never granted another interview, before or since. I spoke to him in a conference room at the state penitentiary for nearly two hours. The story he told me was so different in almost every aspect from his 1974 confession that I determined to search for the real truth.

In the course of my research, I interviewed dozens of people—the law enforcement officers who were involved in the case, family members of the victims, weapons experts, and forensic psychiatrists. I traveled to southwestern Nebraska and walked the streets of McCook and the surrounding area. I read newspaper articles that discussed the case and stacks of court documents that the current district judge released to me. I wrestled with the discrepancies between Harold Nokes's two stories—his 1974 confession and what he told me decades later at the penitentiary—finally reaching some of my own conclusions about what happened that September night.

I do not think Harold Nokes told the truth in 1974. I do not think he told me the truth when I talked to him at the penitentiary. I think his wife was much more of a participant in the killings and their aftermath than Nokes claimed. I do not think that we will ever know with certainty how and why Harold and Ena Nokes acted. But we do know that Edwin and Wilma Hoyt are dead and that Nokes admitted to killing them. I have tried to point the way, so that each reader may decide for himself or herself what really happened that September night so long ago.

ACKNOWLEDGMENTS

I am indebted to the following persons for their valued assistance on this book: the late Paul Douglas, Judge David Urbom, Lannie Roblee, Owen and Donna Elmer, Jerry Ann Hoyt, Toney Redman, Bob Sawdon Jr., Bridget Barry, Sabrina Ehmke Sergeant, Bill Wieland, Sam Vam Pelt, Cloyd Clark, Jim and Kathryn Bellman, Rich and Joan Kopf, John Wunder, Dick Hove, Jim Cada, John Hewitt, Shawn Renner, DeWayne Hein, Ron Olberding, Jack Battershell, Jerry Smith, Kim Corgan, Win Barber, and Mrs. Pat Sexton. Their aid and encouragement sustained me over the many years that I devoted to this project.

For her unflagging attention to detail, proofreading, grammatical instruction, and the typing of draft after draft after draft, I am indebted to my wife Marjorie for the finished product and for much else. It is a debt I will never be able to repay.

IN COLD STORAGE

Introduction

Located in the remote and hilly land north and west of Cambridge, Nebraska, in the southwestern quarter of the state is Harry Strunk Lake, a mecca for Nebraska fishermen. The lake, a Bureau of Reclamation flood-control reservoir, is near the southern edge of Frontier County and is a bright spot in an otherwise lonely and rugged landscape.

On Wednesday, October 3, 1973, a strong wind pushed waves across the lake and up onto the rocks that covered the face of Medicine Creek Dam. Dean McQuiety, a farmer from near Cambridge who loved to fish, was walking along the dam that day looking for carp. As he neared the west end of the dam, he spotted something in the water. Looking closer, he saw a human foot bobbing against the rocks. Alarmed, McQuiety scanned the area. Seeing no one and nothing out of the ordinary, he bent down and gingerly pulled the foot out of the water. Leaving the disturbing find on the rocks, he hurried to the lake office of Tim Jackson, the lake supervisor, with the news of the macabre discovery. McQuiety waited nervously while Jackson telephoned the Bureau of Reclamation office in McCook, twenty-five miles to the southwest, and the Frontier County Sheriff's Office in Curtis, some thirty miles to the north, advising them both of the discovery.

While they awaited the arrival of the sheriff, Jackson and McQuiety returned to the lake to search the area. As they walked along the dam, Jackson saw an object in the water and pulled it onto the rocks. It was the right arm of a female, with the hand attached. On the third finger of the hand was a ring studded with five varicolored stones.

Sheriff Lannie Roblee of Frontier County soon arrived at the lake and was shortly thereafter joined by two of his deputies. Sgt. Merle Divis of Holdrege, a member of the Nebraska State Patrol's Criminal Investigation Section, and Robert Lochenour, a mortician from Cambridge, also arrived at the lake to assist in the investigation. Robert Sawdon, a private investigator from Lincoln, also joined the group. Sawdon had been hired a few days earlier by the family of Edwin and Wilma Hoyt of Culbertson, who had been missing from their home since September 23.

The men spent the late afternoon scouring the area. They discovered additional human remains on the rocks of the dam, in the water in front of the dam, and along the shoreline. The searchers compiled a grisly inventory:

1. Right breast (female).
2. Left foot (apparently female).
3. A large piece of skin, approximately four inches by seven inches with what appeared to be a bullet hole in it. The hole was edged with black, which appeared to be powder burns.
4. Right lower forearm and hand (female), with a ring on the third finger containing five varicolored stones.
5. A part of the right pelvic bone (apparently female).
6. Lower half of a femur (sex not known).
7. Left breast, six ribs, and part of a sternum (female).
8. Upper half of a lower leg, from just below the knee to the ankle (sex not known).
9. Left lower forearm and hand (female), with an engagement ring and a wedding band on the third finger.

One of Roblee's deputies took numerous photographs of each body part and the location in which each part was found. Dusk arrived around 6:00 p.m., and the search was called off until the next day.

Robert Lochenour removed the sodden and severed remains to his mortuary in Cambridge. As he unpacked the findings from the lake, Sergeant Divis took fingerprint impressions of the fingers on both the left and right hands and removed the rings, marking them as evidence. Dr. C. G. Gross, a Cambridge physician, arrived at the mortuary to assist in identifying the various body parts, and the three men carried out a thorough examination of the disturbing collection. The piece of skin with the apparent bullet hole elicited a great deal of attention. The sheriff's deputy photographed the skin, along with the other body parts, as they were laid out on a table in the mortuary's embalming area. Those present speculated that the hole indicated a gunshot wound, and it was measured in an effort to determine the gun's caliber.

Grass, milkweed seeds, cockleburs, and other foreign matter were found on several of the parts, consistent with immersion in a lake in an agricultural area. Fibrous matter on the left forearm and the hand bearing the engagement and wedding rings indicated that the part might have been wrapped in paper, according to Dr. Gross; the material was bagged as evidence by a deputy. After examining the body parts, Dr. Gross stated that dissection had taken place after death as there was no indication of any blood in the veins at the location of the cuts.

All those present were stunned at their findings. This had been no accident. This was the work of a monster. What sort of fiend was loose in southwestern Nebraska?

Two days later, on October 5, 1973, the inventory of human

remains grew after fishermen found two additional body parts washed up on the beach on the northeastern side of the lake. Sheriff's deputies, already at the lake that morning to continue the investigation, proceeded to the discovery site and collected parts ten and eleven, which were photographed by a deputy and removed to the mortuary by Lochenour.

Body part ten, believed to be from a female, was long and irregular in shape and included part of the shoulder, five ribs, and skin and flesh from the upper back. At the mortuary Dr. Gross, again called on for assistance, pointed out what appeared to be a bullet hole that had pierced the flesh and may have broken off a portion of a rib as it entered the body. Gross believed that body part eleven was part of the stomach area of a male body, including the navel. Gross also noticed the presence of fibrous matter resembling paper on body part ten. Gross removed the matter, which the deputy then sealed and marked as evidence.

The following morning, October 6, Tim Jackson, the lake supervisor, discovered another body part on the rocks of the dam. He called Sheriff Roblee, who took the part to the mortuary, where it was assigned number twelve and identified as a forearm by Dr. Gross.

The local press trumpeted the sensational discoveries and speculated about the identities of the victims. Law enforcement officers, on the other hand, were quite sure about the identities of the victims, as the rings removed by Sergeant Divis had been positively identified on the evening of October 3. The law officers, though, were reluctant to release the identity of the victims as Edwin and Wilma Hoyt until after more extensive investigation.

McCook was shocked at the discovery of the bodies. The small town was still reeling from the suspicious death of resident Ida Fitzgibbons in the spring of 1973, and the double murder threw the town into a panic. Some residents believed the murders were part of a satanic plot; football players at the junior college were suspected of all kinds of criminal activity; while rumors of wife swapping, where husbands threw their car keys in a pile and their wives went home with the man picking up the keys, shot through the town like electrical currents.

McCook feared a deranged lunatic was loose in the community. Parents began picking up their children at school rather than letting them walk home. Doors that always had been left open were locked. At one of the Nokeses' neighboring households, the husband had to go out of town during the furor. He told his wife that if she were afraid, she should spend the night with Harold and Ena because they would protect her. She did.

A run on handguns, especially by older citizens, cleaned out all of McCook's sporting-goods shops. The *McCook Gazette*, the town's only newspaper, quoted a store clerk who said on October 6 that he could have sold a dozen more handguns that day if he had had them in stock. The *Gazette* also reported that one elderly couple married in an attempt to protect each other (they later separated when the identity of the murderer became known). The *Gazette*'s daily circulation rose from nine thousand to eleven thousand, as local residents tried to stay informed of the latest developments.

Edwin and Wilma Hoyt were a well-known and well-liked couple who worked in McCook and lived on their farm near Culbertson, eleven miles west of McCook. They had not been seen or heard from by anyone since the evening of September 23, and their family had alerted law enforcement shortly after their disappearance.

Both of the Hoyts' daughters had searched the farm on foot, on horseback, and by airplane. A son and his family came from Wisconsin to assist while a son in the navy in South Carolina arrived home on compassionate leave. Edwin Hoyt's brother, a retired air force officer, came from his home in California. The family placed information about the disappearance in the *McCook Gazette*, on television, and on radio stations to alert area residents. After receiving no information or leads, the family decided to hire a private investigator and engaged Robert Sawdon, a former high-ranking police detective in Lincoln who had recently retired.

Sawdon arrived in McCook on October 1, and immediately plunged into the case. He had several extensive conversations with family members and learned a great deal of information, including that the state patrol had investigated one of the Hoyt daughters earlier in the summer. He became aware of animosity between Edwin Hoyt and Harold Nokes and wondered about the role, if any, that Nokes might have played.

On the evening of October 3, after the initial discovery of the remains, Divis, Sawdon, Sheriff Roblee, and several state patrol officers took the rings that had been removed from the discovered hands to the state patrol office in McCook. A McCook jeweler was called to the office and identified the ring with five colored stones as a ring he had made for Wilma Hoyt. After the jeweler's identification, Donna Elmer, the elder of the Hoyt daughters, and her husband Owen were called to the office and told of the discovery of the rings. Sawdon and Roblee explained the discovery of the remains. Sergeant Divis showed the rings to Donna Elmer, and she identified them as belonging to her mother.

1

The Place

The state of Nebraska encompasses a vast area. Though not as large as Texas or Alaska or Montana, it would still take a long time to walk the 450 miles from east to west. Its rolling hills, golden wheat fields, and verdant cornfields fill up almost eighty thousand square miles. Travelers crossing the state on Interstate 80 may think Nebraska is flat. But it is not. The state rises gradually from the Missouri River, which forms the eastern border, to the high plains of its western border with Wyoming, gaining almost 4,600 feet in elevation on the way. Before Hawaii and Alaska became states, Nebraska boosters claimed Nebraska was the geographical center of the United States.

Travelers flying over Nebraska are provided with a bird's-eye view of huge circles imprinted on the state's landscape. The circles mark the thousands of center-pivot irrigation systems that contribute so much to the bonanza that is Nebraska farming.

Nebraska's population today is well under 2 million. About half of the state's residents live in Omaha and Lincoln, the state's only two cities of any size, and their surrounding suburban areas, all located within fifty miles of the eastern border. The western four hundred miles of Nebraska are dotted with small towns, farms, and ranches.

In far western Nebraska, people are isolated. Farmsteads and ranch homes are often located miles from each other.

The most prevalent signs of civilization are grain elevators, which tower over western towns and villages and provide solitary landmarks on the horizon.

McCook, the county seat of Red Willow County, is today a bustling community of nearly eight thousand people. The town has remained nearly static in size over the past forty years; in the 1970 census its population was 8,285. The only town of significant size in the southwestern corner of the state, McCook is situated seventy-five miles east of the Colorado-Nebraska border on U.S. Highways 6 and 34, two of the major highways spanning the state from east to west. Located fourteen miles north of the Nebraska-Kansas state line, the town is a trade center for a large area, including part of northwestern Kansas.

McCook, named for Alexander McCook, a Union general in the Civil War, is an important city on the Burlington Northern Santa Fe Railroad, which expanded into the Republican River valley in the late 1870s, on its way to Denver. The railroad was instrumental in the settlement of the Republican valley, enticing European immigrants into the area with fanciful tales published in newspapers and pamphlets all over Europe of an agricultural paradise waiting to yield its bounty. Despite their disillusionment in finding something less than a modern Eden, many of the immigrants remained and put down roots. The railroad has been a major employer and significant presence in McCook ever since.

McCook stretches north from the Burlington North ern Santa Fe railroad tracks. The town's principal street—originally called Main Street but now Norris Avenue, to honor the late senator George W. Norris, a McCook resident and one of Nebraska's most distinguished citizens—runs in a north-south direction. Highways 6 and 34, the most significant traffic arteries in the region, parallel the north side of the tracks and form the southern edge of downtown.

Two- and three-story buildings line both sides of Norris Avenue through downtown McCook. The majority of the buildings are outdated; there is no modern construction here. Some are empty. Many have been converted to something other than their original use. A bakery and café, a Mexican restaurant, the county historical society greet passersby. The town's last hotel, now in the throes of conversion to some other residential use, is the largest structure on the west side of the street. A short distance to the north, the county courthouse, a boxy tan three-story structure of little architectural merit, occupies the northwest corner of a Norris Avenue intersection. Past the downtown area, the city changes and improves. A short walk north of the courthouse is a residential neighborhood where McCook proudly claims one of the most impressive structures in the state, a home still known as "the Sutton House."

Sutton, a pioneer McCook jeweler, built a small structure on the property in the 1890s; his wife, who had somewhat grandiose ideas for housing in southwestern Nebraska, wanted more. She contacted noted Chicago architect Frank Lloyd Wright; during the first decade of the twentieth century, Wright designed and the Suttons built a magnificent prairie-style home on the property, razing the previous home. The home cost $10,000 in 1908, which infuriated Sutton, who had relied upon Wright's estimate that it could be built for less. Today, the construction would cost more than a million dollars, as inflation has elevated the cost of living some 2,200 percent since 1910.

After the death of the Suttons, the home passed into the hands of several owners, who modified it extensively. Its current owners, however, recognizing its merit, have restored it to its original grandeur; it remains a private residence and a source of civic pride.

Farther north of the Sutton House on Norris Avenue is the two-story white frame home of the late George W. Norris, a McCook resident for his entire forty-year career in the U.S. House and Senate. And Norris Avenue recognizes his service. Norris is generally acknowledged to have been one of the greatest senators to ever hold that office. He is widely recognized as the father of Nebraska's unique unicameral legislature, which he fostered as an exercise in good government. His home is now maintained and operated by the Nebraska State Historical Society. A pleasant park occupies the east side of Norris across the street from his home.

Much as Ohio and Virginia consider themselves "the cradle of presidents," McCook thinks of itself as the mother of governors. Three of Nebraska's governors—Ralph Brooks, Frank Morrison, and E. Benjamin Nelson—spent significant time in McCook. Morrison was a lawyer, and Brooks was the superintendent of schools in McCook. Though Nelson spent only his boyhood in the town, he remained a tireless advocate for McCook after he reached the U.S. Senate. In accord with the municipal penchant for recognizing the prowess of its native sons, all of these men's homes are outfitted with historical markers. No such marker, however, designates the home of Harold Nokes.

Rolling hills and weathered canyons eroded by wind and water surround McCook. Too difficult to cultivate, much of the land is used as pasture.

What few trees there are, mostly cottonwoods, line the banks of the region's streams and rivers. Many of the pastures and canyons are dotted with scruffy red cedars, a tree that most farmers and ranchers view as an invasive pest.

The Republican River, which flows eastward out of Colorado, at McCook is a puny little water course. Democrats say that it is a toss-up whether the Republican was so named because it was so shallow or so crooked. The water moving down the stream bed past the southern edge of McCook is about thirty feet wide, but it occupies only part of a much wider channel now nearly choked with weeds and grasses. Irrigation farther west in Nebraska and Colorado has siphoned off most of the water in the river bed by the time it gets to McCook. But that was not always the case. In late May of 1935, after a widespread downpour that averaged nine inches across a large area of the watershed, a wall of water up to eight feet high swept down the channel, expanding the usually sedate river from a width of one hundred yards to an uncontrolled monster over two miles wide. In the event, 113 people lost their lives. Property damage ran into the millions, with 341 miles of highway and 307 bridges destroyed.

Carl T. Curtis, then the U.S. congressman from the district and later a U.S. senator, worked zealously to include the Republican River valley in the flood-control provisions of the Pick-Sloan Missouri Basin Program. Dams were constructed to control the feast or famine presence of water in the Upper Missouri and its tributaries to manage the flow of rivers. The Frenchman-Cambridge division of the Pick-Sloan Plan included a number of dams near McCook, water courses that are tributaries of the Republican River.

The U.S. Bureau of Reclamation supervised the construction of the Medicine Creek Dam, an impoundment in the hills two miles west and seven miles north of Cambridge, Nebraska, twenty-five miles northeast of McCook. The dam, built in 1949, is an earthen fill 165 feet high and over a mile long, lined all along its face with rock riprap. The lake created by the dam is named Harry Strunk Lake, after the irascible but public-spirited publisher of the *McCook Gazette*, who was a prodigious promoter of water projects in the area. Covering a surface area of 1,850 acres, with twenty-nine miles of shoreline, the reservoir is a heavily used recreation spot, drawing boaters and fishermen from a large area of southwest Nebraska.

Agriculture is critical to the economic well-being of the Republican valley, and Strunk Lake irrigates some 56,000 acres. The ubiquitous center pivot irrigation systems, now seen almost everywhere in the rough land around McCook, were just beginning to be utilized in the 1960s and 1970s, following their invention in the late 1940s. Corn, wheat, and grain sorghum were the principal Republican valley crops in the seventies and still are today. Cornstalks stand silent sentinel over the area, looking in the fall for all the world like China's terra-cotta soldiers.

In the 1970s the small towns in the area were hanging on by their fingertips. As populations shrank, businesses and schools closed. In 1920 there were 7,264 school districts in Nebraska's ninety-three counties. By 1953, when the legislature passed a mandatory consolidation bill, the number was 5,983. By 1973 it had shrunk to 1,287. When small towns lost their schools through consolidation, they lost much of the reason for their existence. The abandonment of branch lines by all the major railroads in Nebraska, lines that before World War II had served virtually every whistle stop in the state, hastened the demise of small towns. The railroads desired better operating efficiency, pleading poverty and the growth of truck competition; Nebraska's Railway Commission, now styled the Public Service Commission, granted the petitions to abandon service.

As small-town economies began to falter, the young and the more aggressive began to gravitate toward larger towns. If a town could not keep at least a café and a tavern open, it was doomed. Danbury—where both Harold Nokes and his wife, Ena, attended high school—is some twenty miles south and east of McCook, a mile from the Nebraska-Kansas border. Its current population is 101. Its population in 1940—before the Nokeses finished school, married, and left town—was 236. The decline reveals both the exodus and the impact of school consolidation and the lure of jobs and activity in McCook.

For years, social life in small towns revolved around the churches. Bible classes, ladies' circles, and covered-dish suppers furnished an acceptable forum of social activity. People knew their fellow townsmen well, and fear of public condemnation kept all but the most adventurous in line. These rural communities appeared staid and circumspect, but beneath the veneer of respectability, much activity was beyond the pale.

In 1973 a conservative Republican represented Nebraska's Third Congressional District, which encompasses the western two-thirds of the state. In the U.S. House and Senate, Nebraskans were conservative, and so was the majority of the state legislature. The Third District can still be counted on almost always to select rigidly conservative political figures who reflect the views of their constituents, for various offices throughout the district. It is ironic that George Norris, the hero of McCook, was a liberal throughout his congressional career and won his last Senate election in 1936 as an Independent.

Women were an integral part of the workforce both on farms and on ranches in southwestern Nebraska, but in 1973 there was only one female lawyer in McCook, no female doctors, and only a few women business owners or public officials. Divorce was frowned upon, because cruelty and adultery were virtually the only recognized grounds, and divorced women often carried a stigma. Nebraska did not adopt no-fault divorce until 1972, after which divorces burgeoned.

The people of McCook received their news from the *McCook Gazette*. The *Gazette* was a far cry from a metropolitan paper and made no pretenses that it was. It covered local news vigilantly, reporting on the successes and pitfalls of local businesses and area farmers and recounting stories of social activities in McCook and the surrounding area. In short, it was the consummate small-town newspaper.

During the summer of 1973 in McCook, several items of note appeared very briefly in the *Gazette*, although their significance was not to become apparent until later. On July 13 a story on an inside page briefly indicated that the Sheriff's Office and the state patrol were investigating the appearance of obscene messages about a McCook woman that had appeared on road signs, bridges, park benches, and other highway structures in the region. And on August 31 a very brief paragraph of local news indicated that deputy sheriff Don Haegen was resigning October 1 and that state patrolman Bill Tumblin was resigning effective September 1.

The *Gazette* announced that on September 15 Dewayne Hein, a former McCook resident and backfield star on the 1960 champions, entered into his second marriage in Yuma, Colorado. The story reported that Hein's young daughters, Brenda and Angela, were candle lighters. He and his first wife, Kay Hoyt, had divorced in 1971. Kay was the daughter of Edwin and Wilma Hoyt.

2

The People

Harold DeWayne Nokes was born April 19, 1928. The woman who would become his wife, Ena Nadine Ambler, was born November 6, 1929. Both lived all their formative years in Danbury, Nebraska. They were married April 26, 1946, when Harold was eighteen and Ena sixteen. Ena was one month pregnant at the time. Harold graduated from high school in Danbury in 1946, but Ena never received her diploma, dropping out after her junior year because of the marriage and pregnancy.

Harold was tall—six feet two inches—and well muscled, with a shock of thick dark hair. He was a capable athlete and was selected as second team all-conference in basketball, although the conference was of a somewhat lesser caliber than those including the state's larger cities. He was taciturn, hardworking during and after school, friendly, and well liked by his peers.

No one could describe Ena as tall. Seeing the Nokeses walking together evoked comparisons with Mutt and Jeff, the old comic characters. Ena was barely five feet tall but trim and attractive.

Ena determined early on that Harold's gene pool deserved close inspection. One of Ena's classmates said Ena chased Harold all through high school. They speculated her pregnancy involved a certain willingness on her part to yield to Harold's advances, in the hope that marriage might be in the offing. Perhaps she believed it would be a ticket out of Danbury.

The only institution of higher learning in the general area of Danbury was McCook Junior College, a two-year school known primarily for having introduced a group of reputedly thuggish football players into the area. There were no other colleges within easy driving distance, so students could not commute to college classes. The cost of tuition, books, and room and board at any of the colleges in central and eastern Nebraska must have seemed a fantasy to those eking out a hardscrabble existence in southwestern rural Nebraska. In any event, neither Harold nor Ena entertained thoughts of campus life.

Harold was the youngest of four children. At various times during Harold's youth and adulthood, his father, Leslie E. Nokes, was a county commissioner (commissioners are the governing body of a county) of Red Willow County and the Red Willow County assessor. Upon graduation from high school in 1946, Harold went to work for the county, operating a road maintainer used to care for the county's rural roads. He held that job for about six months and then served temporarily in North Platte, Nebraska, a larger city some seventy miles north of McCook, where he worked as a telephone caller for the Union Pacific railroad for two months, calling railroad crews to report for duty. After the birth of their daughter on December 19, 1946, Harold and Ena moved to Denver, where he worked for the Public Service Company of Colorado for three months. But Denver's lights were not as bright in 1947 as they are now, and the young couple opted to return to the ills they knew, rather than to stay in an alien world. The Nokeses went back to Danbury, where they bought a small café and Harold resumed the road maintainer operation.

After a year in the café business in Danbury, Harold and Ena moved to McCook, where they purchased the Moffit Café, which they operated until selling the business in 1956. The purchaser, however, was unable to make the contract payments, so the Nokeses regained ownership of the café and operated it until 1959, when they sold it again, this time successfully. During their years of café operations, Harold and Ena were responsible for all aspects of the business, including butchering and meat preparation as well as washing and cleaning and waiting tables. A second child was born in McCook to the couple on February 14, 1950.

After selling the café, Harold went to work as a fireman on the Burlington Northern Railroad, operating out of McCook on an as-needed basis on what is known even today as the "extra board" rather than as part of an established crew. Late in 1964 the Burlington Northern eliminated the position of fireman on all its train crews in its continuing battle to lower labor costs, costing Harold his job. Harold soon went to work for the Nebraska Department of Roads in McCook. Before long, he rose to the position of foreman of the road crews, a job he still held in 1973. The job included road maintenance and repair as well as the oversight of bridges, rest areas, road signs, and other road-construction projects.

After the sale of the McCook café, Ena began working for Harold's father in the office of the Red Willow County assessor, where, according to many courthouse occupants, she was an exemplary employee. However, she has also been described by many as cold, calculating, and aloof. When Harold's father retired as assessor, Ena hoped to be appointed to replace him. But the Red Willow County Board appointed another, believing Ena lacked the public relations skills to fill a position that was sometimes adversarial. Even though she was extremely capable, Ena was not outgoing and did not convey a sense of compassionate interest in taxpayers. After leaving the assessor's office, Ena found a job with the McCook Public Schools as a secretary and business manager. She was employed there in 1973.

At the time of the murders, Ena was almost forty-four and sported a 1970s bouffant hairdo. Gravity had begun to give her body a slightly dumpy cast, and her wardrobe was small-town dowdy. Harold, aged forty-five, was still tall and well built and possessed a full head of hair not yet invaded by gray. His outdoor work had given him a bronzed and slightly weather-beaten countenance, and his black horn-rimmed glasses lent him a slightly owlish look. Throughout his youth and into his adult years, Harold was a dedicated hunter and fisherman. He was well versed in the use of guns, as was Ena, and was a good shot. He belonged to several gun-related groups, and he also enjoyed fishing, camping, and boating, the consummate outdoorsman. Ena shared his enthusiasm for the outdoors and was described by a high school classmate, Richard Remington, as being "able to shoot the eye out of a hawk." Aside from their hunting and camping companions, the Nokeses were described by a McCook neighbor as a quiet couple who kept "pretty much to themselves." They appeared to be well liked and well thought of in the community.

Edwin and Wilma Hoyt lived in the McCook area all their lives. Edwin was born on a farm near Culbertson, southwest of McCook on January 18, 1918. He attended high school in McCook, graduating in 1935, and was an all-conference guard on the McCook High football team, in a conference substantially more demanding than Harold Nokes's conference in Danbury. He had a somewhat squat but very powerful physique.

After graduation, Edwin attended Barnes Business College

in Denver, Colorado, for a year and then returned to farm with his father near Culbertson. He continued farming on a part-time basis for the rest of his life. He was described by his banker as being a hardworking but not particularly capable farmer. He worked for a time for his son-in-law, Owen Elmer, at the latter's fuel and fertilizer business in Indianola, just east of McCook; at the time of his death, and for several years preceding it, he was employed by Volz Plumbing Company in McCook. Edwin Hoyt had no formal training as a plumber and was not licensed, but he was diligent and capable. He began as a plumber's assistant but caught on quickly and progressed to the point where he could handle projects on his own, even though his work had to be inspected by one of the licensed plumbers at Volz.

Edwin Hoyt was well regarded by his employers both for his work ethic and for his personality. Edwin was balding and wore glasses and a big smile. Although he was reputed to have a fiery temper, he kept it in check. He had two brothers—Marvin, who farmed near Edwin, and Thurber, an air force colonel at Castle Air Force Base in California. A sister lived at Bridgeport in the far western portion of the Nebraska panhandle.

Edwin Hoyt was a very social individual, outgoing and fun loving. He had strong opinions on most issues, which he was willing to share without being asked, but was reluctant to discuss his personal life, including his family. Edwin was a master Mason and a member of the York Rite bodies in McCook, and both he and his wife were members of the Eastern Star.

Wilma Mae Joy married Edwin Hoyt in June 1938 in Culbertson, Nebraska. Wilma was born August 23, 1917, one of six children, three boys and three girls, and graduated from Culbertson High School.

Wilma began her post–high school career with the telephone company in Culbertson and, at the time of her death, was working as a salesperson at DeGroff's Department Store in McCook.

After their marriage, the Hoyts farmed near Culbertson until their children reached school age, at which time the Hoyts bought and remodeled an old two-story house in Culbertson. The family lived in town during the school year so the children could attend the Culbertson schools; in the summer, they resumed residence on the farm.

In 1953 Homer Hoyt, Edwin's father, suffered a stroke and, unable to continue farming, purchased a home in McCook and moved to town. Edwin bought his father's farm, located just south and west of McCook, and moved his family there so his children could attend high school in McCook, as he had done. After all five of the Hoyt children had graduated from high school, the Hoyts sold the farm and moved back to a family farm, the Bailey place, near Culbertson, where they were living in 1973.

Both Edwin and Wilma Hoyt enjoyed social gatherings. They were especially fond of pinochle and attended pinochle parties on weekends, hauling their children along when they were young. The boys would be ensconced in one of the host's beds, the girls in another, until it was time to go home. Both Edwin and Wilma were avid anglers. Neither hunted much, although Edwin had an old rifle and shotgun, as almost all Nebraska farmers do, in order to control scavenging and predatory animals.

The Hoyts had five children during their marriage: Roger, Donna, Kay, Stanley, and Herbert. At the time of the murders, only Donna and Kay lived in the McCook area. Donna and her husband, Owen Elmer, lived in Indianola, just east of McCook; Kay lived in McCook, where she worked as a secretary and bookkeeper for a construction company. Roger, or Whitey as the family called him, lived in Two Rivers, Wisconsin, where he was employed at a nuclear power plant. Stanley was in the U.S. Air Force in Germany, and Herbert was in the navy in South Carolina.

The Hoyts were doting grandparents. They often watched their daughter Kay's children when she was away. On several early Christmas mornings, they drove to Indianola and waited outside the home of Owen and Donna Elmer until the lights in the home went on, so they could be present when the Elmer children saw what gifts Santa had left for them.

Donna attended high school in McCook and spent some time at Nebraska Wesleyan University in Lincoln and at McCook Junior College. She met her husband, Owen Elmer, at a party in McCook, when they were both home from college for the summer. He had graduated from high school in Indianola and then attended the University of Nebraska–Lincoln.

Owen and Donna were married November 1, 1959, and Owen went to work in the family fertilizer and service-station business. The Elmer's had four children, three girls and one boy. A tall, rawboned westerner, Owen and his wife Donna are the only members of the Hoyt family still living in Nebraska, and they manifest the virtues associated with midwestern life—self-reliance and a willingness to help.

Donna, three and a half years older than Kay, was never particularly fond of her younger sister. Sibling rivalry played a part in the antipathy, Donna having been the only girl in the extended Hoyt family until Kay's birth. At the time of the murders, Donna Elmer described her sister, Kay Hein, going by her married name, as being extremely manipulative. At an early age, Kay learned how to work her parents. She claimed allergies that seemed to have no medical foundation. Drying the dishes made her sneeze so frequently that she was unable to continue. Any time that Donna had a significant event in her life, Kay would collapse. When Donna and Owen told Kay of their engagement, Kay swooned, and Mr. and Mrs. Hoyt learned of the engagement at Kay's bedside in the hospital.

Kay was hospitalized twice at a psychiatric hospital in Omaha—once in the spring of 1960, just as she was graduating from high school, and once in 1970, just before the dissolution of her marriage. Both visits were of very short duration, and no hint of mental illness was discovered. She claimed she was depressed, and her parents, acting on the advice of a local doctor, took her to Omaha. Records of the treating physicians in Omaha do not reflect any treatment other than rest; although they do not state that she was malingering, the implication is present. From all outward signs, Kay was the apple of her parent's eye and could do no wrong.

Kay had a normal and busy high school career—band, drama, various clubs—just like hundreds of her contemporaries. But once she received her diploma, things changed.

Kay and DeWayne Hein dated throughout high school and married after they both graduated in 1961. Their senior year they were chosen by popular vote as King and Queen of Hearts at the Valentine's dance. DeWayne, who preferred to be called Duane in high school, was a star running back on the undefeated Bison football team of 1960. He was very popular with his classmates, one of whom described him as, "one of the nicest, most decent guys I have ever known."

3

The Preliminaries

High school romances often do not last. Some nine years after their marriage, the relationship of Kay and DeWayne Hein cooled, and Kay sued for and received a divorce in 1971. Kay related to a young woman who had rented the basement apartment at her home that she and DeWayne entered into the marriage primarily for sexual satisfaction. When pleasure needed to be replaced by mature acceptance of mutual obligations, the marriage fell apart. Kay was extremely forthright in discussing the cause of the breakup. She told friends, and later law enforcement personnel, that DeWayne made no effort to accommodate her sexual needs and desires. She said he was much more interested in hunting and fishing than in spending time with her. She alleged that his interest in only his sexual satisfaction and his obsession with outdoor sports, to the exclusion of her well-being, constituted extreme cruelty. Kay, however, constantly belittled DeWayne during the course of the marriage. Kay Hein's family and virtually all who knew the couple have made it clear that DeWayne Hein was a good man, a good father, and deserving of better treatment than he received from Kay.

Kay and DeWayne Hein had two daughters, Brenda and Angela. After the divorce, Kay was granted custody of the girls. Because Nebraska did not have a no-fault divorce statute in 1971, Kay had to allege and prove acts of extreme cruelty. Her statements about DeWayne's peremptory sexual treatment constituted part of her proof. Kay also told her parents of DeWayne's harsh words directed toward her and her girls, and both of the Hoyts testified at the trial that he verbally abused Kay and her daughters. The Hoyts learned later from DeWayne and the girls that Kay had fabricated the claims. The Hoyts were devastated to learn that they had given false testimony in reliance on what Kay had told them.

After the divorce, DeWayne moved to Yuma, Colorado, where he worked for the Burlington Northern Railroad, and subsequently remarried. During the latter stages of his marriage to Kay, however, DeWayne Hein worked as a laborer on one of the maintenance crews for the Nebraska Department of Roads, a job that brought him into frequent contact with Harold Nokes.

As a result of the men's proximity at work and shared occupational responsibilities, Harold and Ena Nokes and DeWayne and Kay Hein saw each other socially with some degree of frequency during the Hein marriage. Kay and Ena lunched together frequently, as they were both working in downtown McCook. The Nokeses and DeWayne Hein enjoyed hunting, fishing, and camping, although Kay Hein did not relish such outdoor activities. Kay, however, was forming a strong interest in Harold Nokes and was willing to participate in order to be near him. Dancing also appealed to the couples, and at a New Year's Eve dance at the Elks Club in McCook, Kay kissed Harold Nokes at the stroke of midnight on January 1, 1970. New Year's kisses are, and were, quite common in Nebraska and elsewhere, and such an overt act raised few, if any, eyebrows. The passion that led to the kiss, though, was an eye-opener both for the restive young mother and for the man who seemed to her as a middle-aged authority figure.

The couples continued to see each other; although winter is not a propitious time for camping in western Nebraska, hunting, dancing, and card playing are year-round activities.

Not long after the New Year's Eve dance, Harold Nokes received a telephone call from Kay Hein. She told him that she needed to talk to him about an important matter and asked if he would pick her up in his car. He agreed, and they drove a short distance west of McCook, where they almost immediately engaged in frenzied sex in the front seat of his car parked on a quiet road. The only matter of importance was the satisfaction of the libidinous urges of Kay Hein. The die was cast. The lovers embarked on a sexual journey that was to last until the spring of 1973, a journey that occurred with impressive frequency, often two or three times a week.

Kay Hein enjoyed sex and sexual variations very much. Harold Nokes told law enforcement officials that she was a hard woman to satisfy, a fact not too surprising in light of the fifteen-year difference in their ages. Harold, though, did his best, and for a period of some three years, in one way or another, he found ways to do so. He had had an unexpected bonanza dropped into his lap, and he was not one to ignore its benefits.

As the torrid affair surged on, Kay began to fall in love. She repeatedly urged Harold to leave his wife and marry her. She was willing to divorce DeWayne and, in fact, did so. As straying males often do, Harold temporized. This state of affairs lasted for almost two years—she asked, he evaded.

DeWayne Hein slowly began to realize his marriage was in jeopardy. Coworkers had told him that Kay often met Harold Nokes on a road close to her parent's home, and the workers speculated that where there was smoke, there was fire. But DeWayne put the thought out of his mind, not believing the allegations until Kay filed for divorce.

Ena Nokes began to suspect Harold was having an affair but kept her suspicions to herself. Finally, in the late spring of 1972, Harold, who subsequently claimed that he couldn't stand the guilt attendant to cheating on his wife, broke down and confessed the affair to Ena.

Harold may have confessed his sins to Ena simply because he had run out of plausible excuses. Business men, professional men, can conjure up excuses to be absent from home in the evening, sometimes even overnight, but a man charged with keeping the area roads in shape has little that he can do at night, when darkness obscures vision. No meetings, no business trips, no clients to see. Harold must have been something of a Houdini to have managed to carry on an affair of every-week frequency in a town the size of McCook.

The story Harold told Ena must have been compelling. Not only did she forgive him, but she also agreed to turn the other cheek while he continued the affair. After a short time, he persuaded her that sexual bliss would occur if the three of them were to engage in a ménage à trois, a sexual threesome. Ena agreed, although the degree of her initial enthusiasm is hard to quantify. One can understand a willingness to forgive and forget, but to forgive and ignore the continuation of the offending act is unusual. Even more unusual is to agree to become a participant in the act. Harold later stated that Ena agreed to become involved because she did not want to lose him and because she thought that his continued solo relationship with his mistress might spell the end of the Nokeses' marriage. It may have been possible that even after twenty-five years of marriage, with its many ups and downs, Ena remained so smitten with Harold that she agreed to the threesome out of fear of losing him to a younger woman.

Sexual triangles involving a married couple and a third person are not unheard-of, even if they are not common. Ena might simply have been curious. Because of their frequent activities as couples and their luncheon meetings, she and Kay had become good friends. And as Kay detailed to Bob Sawdon after he had entered the picture in search of her parents, Ena participated in the sexual aspects of the ménage à trois with gusto.

In any event, it seems strange that an errant husband could first confess his infidelity and then convince his wronged spouse to compound the sin by entering into a sexual arrangement with the wrongdoers. But according to Harold Nokes's confession, and confirmed by Kay Hein in her statement to Sawdon and the patrol, that is precisely what occurred.

After Harold and Kay converted their twosome to a threesome by adding Ena, they engaged in group sex with impressive frequency. They were discreet in their activities, and it took the well-developed skills of Bob Sawdon to discover the existence of the affair and how it functioned.

When Edwin and Wilma Hoyt disappeared, Bob Sawdon had no preconceived notion of what might have happened. He was hired to find the missing, and he poured all his energy into locating them. When Sawdon arrived in McCook on October 1, he interviewed the Hoyt family and learned what the patrol knew about Kay and her activities. Sawdon was an old pro in the investigation business, and as the recently retired head of the Criminal Investigation Unit of Lincoln's police department, he had contacts all over the state of Nebraska. After a very short time, he knew everything the state patrol knew; on the evening of October 2, he called Harold Nokes to the state patrol headquarters in McCook and grilled him at length. Harold admitted his affair with Kay, but despite Sawdon's repeated requests, Harold Nokes refused to take a lie detector test and did not discuss Ena's involvement.

Sawdon had learned of Harold Nokes's existence when he reviewed the state patrol report, prepared by W. W. Tumblin in the summer of 1973, concerning obscene messages about Kay Hein that were painted in public places in and around McCook. The *Gazette* had also briefly reported the matter.

Early in June the Red Willow County Sheriff's Office received complaints from two of Kay Hein's alleged sexual partners, men who had enjoyed her favors after the ménage à trois with the Nokeses had ended. The men claimed that their names were being linked with Kay's on obscene messages painted on highway signs, bridges, park benches, rest area shelters, and public restrooms in the McCook area. The Sheriff's Department called the state patrol to assist, and W. W. Tumblin of the patrol and Deputy Don Haegen conducted the investigation. The complainants denied any sexual involvement with Kay, but both were frequently mentioned in the graffiti, which took the form of "Kay Hein is a good fuck. Ask . . ."

During the investigation, Kay was contacted by Tumblin and Haegen and denied any sexual involvement with either of the men mentioned in the graffiti. In truth, she had had sex with both. In discussing possible writers of the graffiti, Kay told Tumblin that she had been friends with Harold Nokes but that they had not had sex. Instead, she named two more of her recent sexual partners and an unsuccessful suitor as possible suspects for the signs. Kay stated that she was unaware of the signs until they were brought to her attention by one of the complainants.

Some of the graffiti appeared in ladies' rooms in rest areas, and Sheriff Lannie Roblee, at the conclusion of the investigation, believed that they were painted by Ena Nokes. Donna Elmer, however, later said that she believed Kay had painted some of the signs, taking a strange and perverse delight in advertising her sexual prowess. In support of her theory, Donna mentioned that soon after she turned down a request by Kay to babysit Kay's children while Kay traveled out of town with one of her admirers, graffiti accusing Donna of immoral behavior appeared on a bridge near the Elmers' home. Donna felt Kay was striking back.

As the investigation proceeded, more obscene messages appeared in Hitchcock County, west of McCook, south of Culbertson, and on county roads around Indianola.

Tumblin began to doubt Kay's previous statement and pressed her as to her sexual activities. During this second questioning, Kay admitted an affair with Harold Nokes. She told Tumblin that the affair began before she and DeWayne divorced and that although she loved Harold, he refused to divorce Ena to marry her. She acknowledged having had sex with one of the men mentioned on the signs, though she denied any involvement with one of the other men. She also named three other local men who had enjoyed her favors.

Kay theorized that one of her sexual partners was the most likely suspect in painting the signs. The patrol then obtained samples of the suspect's handwriting and forwarded them, along with pictures of the signs, to the patrol's documents examiner in Lincoln. He reported that the sample and writings did not match.

Tumblin remained skeptical of Kay's statements and arranged for Kay to take a lie detector test. Sgt. Merle Divis, who would be active in the Hoyt murder investigation, administered the test. After a battery of questions, Divis concluded that Kay was telling the truth about not painting the signs herself and that she correctly named those she had had sex with and those she had not. Though Divis stated in his report to Tumblin that Kay was telling the truth when she said she had not had sex with one of the men named in the graffiti, the man later admitted a long history of sexual encounters with Kay.

Tumblin apparently continued to doubt Kay's story, though from the contents of his report, he made no effort to question Harold Nokes or any of Kay's other sexual partners, relying solely on Kay's statements. It was only after Sawdon began working on the Hoyt case that law enforcement contacted Harold Nokes. Sawdon first came to McCook on October 1 and interviewed Harold the next day.

One retired member of the patrol later said that Tumblin and the deputy from Red Willow County, Don Haegen, who handled the graffiti investigation, were much more interested in Kay Hein than they were in finding the perpetrator. They were rumored to have spent several nights at Kay's house to "protect" her, a gratuitous act since none of the signs had been painted at her house and there had been no harm except to her and the named men's reputations. Such an allegation about the conduct of Tumblin and Haegen is serious and should have led to an investigation. The accusation, though, may well have simply reflected the patrol's feelings about Tumblin after his resignation.

On August 24 Tumblin submitted a report regarding the obscene messages and closed his investigation. Although his report stated that the case remained active, Tumblin resigned a week later on September 1. The files of the patrol and the Red Willow County sheriff have no follow up reports. No arrests were made. No suspects were questioned. Harold Nokes was never interviewed. The Tumblin report has vanished from the files of the patrol, although Paul Douglas, a former attorney general and the special prosecutor in the Hoyt murders, had a copy, which he furnished to the author.

Tumblin may have been so disenchanted with the patrol by the time of the signs investigation that he was simply going through the motions. His issues with the patrol stemmed from his investigation of the death of Ida Fitzgibbons.

On the evening of April 25, 1973, firemen rushed to the McCook home of Ida Fitzgibbons in response to a call from a neighbor reporting smoke and flames. When they arrived, they found the body of the eighty-year-old Fitzgibbons lying near a hole burned in the floor. She was nearly nude, and her lower extremities were burned. Her left leg was broken near the ankle, a clothesline was wrapped three times around her neck and knotted, and she had been stabbed in the chest with a wood-handled knife that remained lodged in her body.

Tumblin was one of the first law enforcement officers to arrive at the scene, as was Deputy Don Haegen; they spent the night examining the house and attending the autopsy, performed by Dr. John Battey, a McCook physician. Tumblin mentioned in a report dated May 14 that Battey concluded after the autopsy that the death was "very obviously" a homicide. The *McCook Gazette* covered its front page on April 26 with the story of the death. Its banner headline read "McCook Woman Murdered-Strangled, Stabbed, House Set on Fire."

Sheriff Jim Short of Red Willow County was out of town the day of Ida Fitzgibbon's death. When he returned to McCook the next day, he removed Haegen from the case. Short cited McCook chief of police William Green's anger that word had leaked that the death was a homicide as reason for Haegen's removal. Chief Green also contacted Lt. Donald Grieb of the patrol's North Platte office the morning of April 26 and asked that Tumblin, too, be removed from any further work on the investigation. Grieb was an experienced criminal investigator, and Grieb agreed to Green's request, which became a source of conflict between Grieb and Tumblin thereafter.

Green then proceeded with the investigation of the death and concluded that it was a suicide.

Red Willow County attorney Clyde Starrett was taken to task by the *Gazette* for the manner in which he tried to determine if the death was in fact a suicide. The *McCook Gazette* printed a number of stories questioning the delay, and on May 11 it ran an editorial titled "How Long? How Long before the People of McCook Get an Answer to the Question on Everyone's Mind for More Than Two Weeks?" The editorial claimed, "The handling of the unfortunate incident may in fact be putting undue strain on many McCookites, particularly the great number of widows who reside alone."

Tumblin felt Green's investigation was seriously defective, simply glossing over the physical evidence and the facts, and made no bones about it then or later. Tumblin prepared a comprehensive report of what he had seen and done in the Fitzgibbons case and furnished copies to Grieb, Green, and Sheriff Jim Short. The Fitzgibbons report, however, was dated May 14, several weeks after the death on April 25, 1973. Neither Tumblin's report nor a report written by Haegen were presented to the coroner's jury called by Starrett in May, nor were either of the men called to testify.

After the jury had deadlocked three against three as to whether the death was a suicide, both the county commissioners of Red Willow County and Starrett, as county attorney, wrote the state patrol, asking them to investigate the death. During the tumult, Tumblin gave the patrol notice on July 31 that he was resigning. Tumblin handed in his badge to the patrol on September 1, as reported by the *McCook Gazette*, and shook the dust of western Nebraska from his feet.

Harold Nokes was never questioned by anyone in law enforcement during the graffiti investigation, even though Kay had admitted her lengthy involvement with him and the cessation of their affair. If Tumblin wrote a report regarding the sign investigation other than his original report of August 24, after he had interviewed Kay, the patrol has not discovered it. Counsel for the patrol stated that Tumblin's personnel file has been discarded, and it is impossible to discover whether patrol supervisors placed any information concerning Tumblin's relationship with Kay in his file.

If Grieb and Tumblin had not been at odds, as a result of Grieb calling Tumblin off the Fitzgibbons death investigation, perhaps Tumblin would have been more diligent in his investigation of the sign painting in the summer of 1973. Had Harold Nokes been queried by the patrol or the county attorney, he would have been on notice that he was a possible suspect in the harassment of Kay Hein. He would have been an absolute fool, knowing he had been the subject of such surveillance and interrogation, to have considered taking any kind of punitive action against Edwin and Wilma Hoyt, or against Kay.

Now aware of what the patrol knew about Kay and her sexual activity, as shown in Tumblin's sign report, Sawdon talked to Kay several times. He deduced that she was not telling the whole truth and that she was trying to protect Harold. He knew he wanted to talk to Harold and did. Both Kay and Harold were also interviewed by Lieutenant Grieb. Nokes detailed for Grieb where and when and how often he and Kay had sex. Kay was very forthcoming about her sexual relations with others but was close mouthed and evasive about her affair with Harold.

Grieb and Sawdon kept each other informed. On October 11, as the investigation moved forward, with a bulldog's tenacity and a bloodhound's nose, Sawdon went to Kay's home and confronted her. She realized that she could remain silent no longer and told Sawdon about her affair with the

Nokeses. After Kay divulged her story, Sawdon took her to the patrol office, where she repeated the narrative to a stenographer. Grieb then arranged for Harold and Ena to be brought to the patrol office. Sawdon separated Harold and Ena and questioned Harold first. After hearing the facts of the affair, as Kay had related them, Harold confirmed Kay's account. Kay repeated her story to Grieb, and Grieb secured Harold's assent that the story was correct.

Sawdon told Ena what Kay had said, then brought Kay into the room to repeat the story. Ena never flinched. She remained cold, calm, and defiant, telling Sawdon that he could not prove any of Kay's story. Grieb then confronted Ena with Harold and told Harold to repeat to Ena what he had told Grieb about the affair. Harold refused to do so, telling Grieb that he did not recall telling him any of that story. Grieb removed Harold from Ena's presence and grilled him as to why he would not tell Ena what he had confessed about the affair. Harold countered that he thought Grieb had doublecrossed him. But he was willing, at that juncture, to reaffirm to Grieb Kay's story as to the formation and continuation of the affair. The story was compelling.

As Kay told it, on or about the Fourth of July, 1972, Harold Nokes called Kay and told her that he and Ena were going to Lake McConaughy, near Ogallala, Nebraska, to fish. Ogallala is about 110 miles north and west of McCook, and McConaughy is Nebraska's largest lake, a paradise for boaters and fishermen. Harold told Kay that she was welcome to join him and Ena, but the cabin in which they would be staying had only one bed. He and Kay had previously discussed the possibility of including Ena in the affair, and now he asked if she would be willing to come to their home and engage in a three-party sexual relationship, a prelude to the fishing trip.

Kay, who later admitted to Sawdon that she would do anything to win Harold's love and who wanted to continue their sexual arrangement, agreed. She went to the Nokeses' home later that evening, taking a nightgown and her two young daughters with her and putting them to bed in the Nokeses' spare bedroom.

The start of the ménage à trois, detailed by Kay to Bob Sawdon on October 11, shortly after the murders of her parents had been discovered, is riveting:

Q. Now first of all, Ena was there when you arrived at the house?

A. Yes.

Q. Did you and Ena and he discuss this at all before you actually went to bed?

A. Yes, she said that she knew how he felt and she was sure that she knew how I felt and she didn't want to lose him.

Q. Now was she referring to how he felt about you and how you felt about him?

A. Yes

Q. Now you had been having an affair with him prior to this time, is that true?

A. Yes.

Q. Had you been having intercourse with him?

A. Yes.

Q. Over what period of time prior to July, 1972?

A. It would have been about a year, maybe a little longer.

Q. Was this with knowledge of his wife Ena that you and he were having this affair?

A. No, no one knew.

With prompting from Sawdon, Kay described in graphic detail the activities of that night and of the duration of the ménage à trois.

Kay detailed at length the positions the parties assumed and the cunnilingus the women performed on each other while one of the pair was having intercourse with Harold. He engaged in vaginal and anal intercourse with them, and each performed oral sex on him. Harold was the ringmaster, suggesting various sexual positions, and displayed an innovative list of activities.

During his questioning of Kay, Sawdon elicited a great deal more information about the sexual aspects of the affair than was necessary, even in the name of careful investigative work. Perhaps the details appealed to his prurient interest. Perhaps he felt descriptions of steamy sex in a transcript would make entertaining reading in station houses and patrol offices across Nebraska. Whatever the reason, what he managed to get from Kay could be used as a primer for anyone hoping or planning to engage in three-way sex. In today's more circumscribed climate, a complaint by Kay about the invasive nature of his interrogation might well interest a plaintiff's lawyer or the ACLU, even though Sawdon was working for the family and Kay wished to cooperate in finding whoever killed her parents and mutilated their bodies.

The experiment at the Nokeses' house evidently proved satisfactory. The parties went to a cabin at LeMoyne, on the shore of Lake McConaughy, for the Fourth of July weekend and repeated the performance there. The parties met two or three times a week thereafter in such diverse locales as the Nokeses' home; the Hein home; North Platte; Harry Strunk Lake, near Cambridge; and Lincoln.

The activity was obviously pleasurable to all of the actors, but to Harold it must have seemed like a dream come true, every adolescent's fantasy of romping with two women. Dreams coming true, fantasies being fulfilled, were not a part of life in Danbury or McCook.

The trio continued their sexual activity without cessation until March of 1973. However, the Nokeses had noticed a certain diminishment in Kay Hein's enthusiasm beginning in the late fall of 1972, when she had suffered a concussion after hitting her head on an open cupboard door in her kitchen. Her parents took her to a hospital in McCook and then to a clinic in Holdrege, Nebraska. Although she resumed the ménage à trois after her return to McCook, her attitude was different.

During the course of Kay's involvement with Nokeses, Kay's parents had become worried about Harold's influence over her. At one point, Harold loaned her six hundred dollars to buy a car. When Kay fell ill with a bad cold, instead of asking her parents for help, she allowed the Nokeses to assist her and stayed at their home. The Hoyts' concerns about the influence the Nokeses exercised on Kay were soon to have an even stronger factual foundation.

In March of 1973, the Nokeses and Kay traveled to Kansas City, Missouri, staying overnight on their return in Salina, Kansas. They went dancing after dinner, and Kay complained to Harold that he spent too much time dancing with Ena and not enough time dancing with and paying attention to her. It must have become increasingly apparent to Kay that Harold was enjoying the affair but had no intention of leaving Ena. When they returned to the motel, her temper flared, and she called Harold a son of a bitch.

Harold had a temper of his own, and he slapped Kay, knocking her down and giving her a black eye. She demanded to return to McCook immediately, and the parties left at once, driving all night to reach home. For all intents and purposes, that was the end of the affair.

Kay notified the Nokeses that the party was over, and despite frequent and impassioned importuning by both

Harold and Ena, she remained adamant. Kay told Sawdon of her decision:

Q. Why did you stop participating in these sex activities with the Nokes?

A. I couldn't take it anymore. I loved Harold and I was so sure that Ena wouldn't go for this and I was so sure that he would leave her and I just wanted to be a person, a whole person and he didn't want that. I wanted him alone.

Q. You didn't want to share him with his wife?

A. No, I tried, I really tried.

Q. Kay, was there any problem or disagreement when you chose to terminate this activity.

A. He said I would be sorry some day.

Q. What reaction did you get from Ena Nokes?

A. She thought I was terrible.

Q. Do you have a feeling of, or any reason to believe that Ena Nokes had any feelings of affection for you in a sexual way?

A. She always said it helped their life an awful lot and that it wasn't the same without me.

The end of the affair was discouraging for the Nokeses, who had found a new excitement in their lives. Despite Kay's insistence that she was finished with the affair, both Harold and Ena tried to persuade Kay to rejoin them.

In April of 1973, while Ena Nokes was talking to Kay on the telephone, Ena noticed that Kay sounded very different; when Harold arrived home from work, they went to Kay's home to check on her. After they arrived, Kay slapped one of her daughters for a minor infraction, and Harold urged her to stop. She became hysterical and threw an empty pill bottle on the floor at the Nokeses' feet. She stuffed a twenty-dollar bill in Harold's shirt pocket and told him to buy flowers from her girls at her funeral. Worried that Kay had taken the pills, Harold called Kay's mother, who called her husband. The Nokeses stayed with Kay until Edwin Hoyt picked up Kay and her children, taking Kay to a clinic in Holdrege.

When Kay returned to McCook after a short visit to a doctor in Holdrege to insure that she had not actually overdosed on pills, she began a determined campaign to satisfy her sexual desires with a variety of men. Her conquests included her employer, a local auto dealer, several members of the construction industry, and one ex-convict. During her questioning by Sawdon, she acknowledged having participated in affairs with seven men during the summer of 1973. Her reasons for the sexual encounters are not known to anyone but her, but it is not unreasonable to suppose that it was an effort to demonstrate to Harold that other men found her attractive, even if he did not. Harold, however, had been trying diligently to convince Kay to resume the triangle, so perhaps Kay was using the affairs as a ploy to make Harold jealous and to persuade him to leave Ena and marry her.

McCook is a small town. Neighbors know what their neighbors are doing, and Kay's small house was cheek by jowl with the houses on either side of her. Harold heard rumors about Kay's promiscuity but continued to implore her to return to the affair. Kay continued to refuse. Angered, he struck back. In May, in the dark of night, Harold poured a powerful weed killer on Kay's front lawn, killing the grass and damaging her shrubs and trees. She was unaware of the identity of the perpetrator, though it's likely she suspected Harold.

Harold told Kay, in one of his frequent cajoling calls, that she would be sorry that she had ended the arrangement. When her lawn was destroyed, she must have been frightened that he was carrying out his threat. He also told her that he had incurred a great deal of expense in taking her on numerous trips, so she brought four hundred dollars in cash to his home. He told her he did not want it, but she refused to take it back.

Harold also told Kay that she was a "two-bit whore" and that she needed a red light on her front porch to advertise her profession. Shortly thereafter, she received a package in the mail. It contained a lightbulb painted red. Harold subsequently admitted sending the package.

Everything that Harold did, every action he took against Kay, revealed the petulance of a denied youth—a willingness to cry, stomp one's feet, and throw a tantrum in order to gain a sought-after objective. He had no idea how to lure her back.

Such behavior was very much out of character for Harold. People found him to be friendly but a bit distant, generally calm and composed. He was well liked and well regarded by those who knew him. His actions in regard to Kay show how deeply he cared for her and how important the affair was to him.

In a desperate attempt to convince Kay to return to the affair, the Nokeses concocted a scheme that they believed would lure her to their house. Their plan succeeded, but with dire consequences for Harold.

One day in June, shortly after noon, Ena Nokes called Kay and told her that she had cut her hand using a box cutter and that she was having trouble bandaging her hand. She asked Kay to come to the Nokeses' home to help her wrap the injury. When Kay arrived, the door was open, and Ena was standing in the living room with her hand wrapped in a towel. When Kay entered the home, Harold, who was standing out of sight behind the door, shut the door.

Ena removed the towel from her hand and admitted that there was no injury and that the call was a ruse. She told Kay that Harold wanted to talk. Ena said she would drive Kay's car to East Ward Elementary School, where Ena worked, and leave it there. No one recalls whether Kay had left the keys in her car or whether Kay handed them to Ena. Why Ena did not stay for the conversation between Harold and Kay and why Kay allowed Ena to drive away in her car is bewildering. So is the fact that Kay, having been tricked, was willing to stay at the Nokeses' home and talk to Harold.

Kay was visibly upset and nervous. Harold acknowledged that they had deceived her but asked her to come with him to the basement, as he had something to show her. When they reached the basement, Harold offered Kay a loaded deer rifle and told her to shoot him, because his life was not worth living without her. Kay refused to accept the rifle and retreated upstairs. Harold followed her into the living room, where they talked for a while. He asked her to engage in sex with him, but she refused. When Harold moved into the kitchen, Kay saw an opportunity to flee. She ran for the door, down the porch steps, and across the street. Harold started after her in hot pursuit, but as he reached the edge of the stoop, he slipped and fell some three feet to the ground below. The fall caused a severe injury to his right shoulder, weakening it and his arm substantially, an injury that still bothers him forty years later.

In spite of the injury, Harold jumped to his feet to pursue the fleeing Kay. He quickly caught her, tearing her dress and bra in the process, and took her back inside the house. Harold yelled at Kay, warning her that the neighbors would certainly talk. Kay became ill, vomited, and passed out. When she regained consciousness, Harold called Ena at the school and told her of his fall. He said he was in severe pain and needed to see a doctor for his shoulder. Harold then made Kay promise to return to the Nokeses' house after he had received medical treatment. Kay agreed, so Harold drove her to her car at East Ward Elementary School, then went to see a doctor. Kay, who had promised to return only to forestall any further action on Harold Nokes's part, drove home and never went back. She never visited the Nokeses again, although Harold called her several times, begging for further contact.

In July of 1973 Harold poured sugar into the gas tank of Kay's car, which was parked in front of her house, causing serious damage to the engine. No evidence exists that shows he took any further action or had any further contact with Kay until September 23.

Sometime during June, Harold stopped to see Edwin Hoyt at the Volz Brothers' plumbing shop, where Edwin worked, and asked how Kay was getting along. Why he did raises a series of questions. Was he trying to show concern? Did he think Edwin Hoyt would tell Kay that Harold was worried about her? Was he fishing for information about what Kay was doing? Edwin was obviously angry with Harold and was curt in his responses. Aware of Kay's four hundred–dollar payment to Harold, Edwin also accused him of blackmailing her. Harold denied the allegations.

4

The Perpetration

In late August 1973 Edwin and Wilma Hoyt set out on a trip
to Germany to see their son Stanley, who was stationed there
in the U.S. Air Force. Stanley Hoyt had married a woman several years his senior who had originally come to the United
States after World War II as a German war bride. Her husband
subsequently deserted her, leaving her with several children,
one of whom was only slightly younger than Stanley. Stanley
felt that his parents and siblings disapproved of his marriage,
a notion that his sister Donna and her husband Owen Elmer
have dismissed as untrue. Stanley had asked to be reassigned
to Germany during his air force service, a venue decidedly
more hospitable to his wife, who had relatives still living in
Germany. The visit of the elder Hoyts to see Stanley and his
family may well have been an effort to alleviate his concerns
about parental disapproval.

Accompanied by Kay and her two daughters, Edwin and
Wilma drove to Two Rivers, Wisconsin, where their son Roger
and his family lived. They left their car at Roger's home and
flew from Chicago to Germany. Kay had planned to visit with
Roger, or Whitey as he was known to the family, for a week
and then return to McCook.

Jerry Anne Hoyt, Roger's wife, had a number of conversations with Wilma Hoyt, both before Wilma and Edwin left
for Germany and after they had returned. Both Jerry Anne
and Donna Elmer have said that Edwin and Wilma Hoyt

were both in a state of perpetual denial concerning Kay, her escapades, and her difficulties. As Jerry Anne put it, "They thought if they didn't talk about it, it didn't happen." Nonetheless, having a friendly and understanding ear available, Mrs. Hoyt did discuss the recent events—the sugar in Kay's gas tank, her ruined lawn, and the graffiti on highway signs. Wilma told Jerry Anne that she did not want to talk about Kay and her problems on the phone, because their farm was on a multiparty rural phone line, where anyone else on the line could listen in. She was especially distressed that she and Edwin had given false testimony against DeWayne Hein in Kay's divorce action because of the lies Kay had told them.

Before arriving in Wisconsin, Wilma Hoyt had written Jerry Anne about Kay and her relationship with Harold and Ena Nokes. She did not talk about sex but about the unhealthy influence the Nokeses had over Kay. Kay had refused to see a doctor in Holdrege, Nebraska, who had been treating her, because the doctor was Harold Nokes's uncle. Wilma said she had never liked or trusted Harold Nokes and did not know how Ena put up with him.

Wilma also wrote that Kay had been a real worry for her and Edwin, that she was dating a contractor in McCook, and that she saw her parents only when she wanted them to babysit or wanted something else from them. The letter made it seem as if Wilma was becoming aware of some of Kay's character flaws and even of her promiscuity.

Such knowledge leads inevitably to the question of why the Hoyts brought Kay and her daughters to Wisconsin with them. It may well be that they thought it advisable to get Kay out of McCook. Indeed, Wilma's letter stated that it would be best if Kay got a job somewhere else. Wilma had also voiced concern for Kay's daughters, and she and Edwin may have decided to give the girls a treat by taking them on a trip.

After Edwin and Wilma had departed for Germany, Kay and Whitey had a furious argument. Kay and Whitey had never been close. He was much closer to Donna and shared her view that Kay manipulated their parents. Whitey chastised Kay for spending so much time with the Nokeses, when she had not been willing to spend equivalent time with DeWayne Hein. Kay placed her face within inches of Whitey's, and he told her that if she moved any closer, he would bite her. She did, and he in turn bit her on the lip. She went upstairs, roused her girls out of bed, and brought them downstairs, telling them she wanted them to see how adults fought. Whitey subsequently told law enforcement officers during the investigation of the Hoyts' disappearance that he was convinced that if Kay had had a gun in her hand, she would have shot him.

After the argument, Kay wanted to drive her parents' car back to Nebraska. She demanded the car keys, but Whitey refused. Instead, he and Jerry Anne put Kay and the girls on Amtrak to return to Nebraska, and the three left before Edwin and Wilma returned from Germany.

Upon the Hoyts' arrival back in the states, they had planned to spend several days with Whitey and Jerry Anne, but Kay called them from McCook and told them she had broken her arm falling off the tailgate of a pickup while feeding Marvin Hoyt's cattle. Marvin, Edwin's brother, farmed near Edwin and had fed Edwin's cattle during the trip to Germany. He then left for Hawaii to celebrate a wedding anniversary. Kay was carrying out some of the feeding duties until Edwin returned. The Hoyt family later learned from Kay's doctor that Kay had not broken her arm, though she insisted she had. To placate her, the doctor wrapped her arm and put it in a soft cast, even though there was no break. However, her phone call to her parents with news of her alleged accident prompted them to cut short their trip and drive back to Nebraska.

Jerry Anne Hoyt, who is on the side of Donna and Owen Elmer in blaming Kay for being the catalyst in the death of the Hoyts, wonders if the phone call was part of a scheme to lure the Hoyts home to face the Nokeses.

The Hoyts returned to McCook on Thursday, September 20. They spent some time catching up with neighbors and family on all that had transpired during their absence, paying bills that had accumulated, and carrying out all the little chores that need to be done when one returns from vacation. On Sunday, September 23, they hosted a family dinner where they related the stories of their travels. Present were Flossie Joy (Wilma Hoyt's mother), Owen and Donna Elmer and their four children, and Kay Hein and her two daughters. The Elmers, their children, and Mrs. Joy left around 4:00 p.m. Kay remained about a half hour longer, as she and her mother attempted to find some old music books Kay wanted for her daughters. Wilma then cleared and washed all the dishes except for the pan used to bake the ham, which was soaking in the sink.

At about 7:30 p.m. the Hoyts received a telephone call from their son Herbert, who was in the U.S. Navy and stationed in Charleston, South Carolina. Both Wilma and Edwin spoke to him during the brief call.

As Edwin and Wilma relaxed at home on the evening of Sunday, September 23, 1973, Harold and Ena Nokes drove from their home in McCook to the Hoyts' farm south of Culbertson, Nebraska, a distance of some fifteen miles. As Harold Nokes stated in his formal confession, he and Ena went to see the Hoyts in an effort to resolve the tension between the two couples resulting from the Hoyts' concern about the Nokeses' influence on Kay.

Why the Nokeses selected that evening for their visit is unknown. Did they know the Hoyts had gone to Germany?

And how would they have known the Hoyts were home alone that evening? Did Kay tell them? Why was it important for them to make amends with the Hoyts? Had they worked things out with Kay, conditioned on a parental blessing?

Although Harold Nokes was in good physical condition, the shoulder injury he had sustained while chasing Kay severely restricted the use of his right arm. According to Harold, because he feared Edwin Hoyt's temper and physical strength, he took with him a loaded .22-caliber Ruger pistol, which he tucked in the waistband of his trousers, where it was concealed by his jacket. Harold had purchased the gun only a few weeks earlier on August 25, from a gun shop in McCook. There was a full clip in the handle of the pistol and a round in the chamber. The safety on the gun was engaged. Harold, an avid hunter, had several rifles and shotguns but had not possessed a handgun until he bought the Ruger. He subsequently maintained, both to Sawdon and later in his confession, that he knew his damaged shoulder would not withstand the recoil of a long gun, and so he bought the pistol for target practice and hunting small game while his wife and son hunted larger quarry. In Nebraska in 1973, between August 25, when Harold Nokes bought the pistol, and September 23, when he used it, the only open hunting season was for cottontail rabbits and squirrels. Therefore, his purchase of the gun for hunting or target shooting was well in advance of any possible hunting trips planned for the fall of 1973.

The conversation between Harold and Ena on that fateful Sunday and on the trip to the Hoyt farm has remained a mystery. Why did they decide to go, and at a late hour? Was it a spur of the moment decision? Did they discuss having Kay call her parents? Did they discuss if Harold should bring the gun? Did Ena even know Harold had the gun with him? Did they make plans about what to do if Edwin Hoyt refused to talk or if he threatened to throw them off his property? Or did they simply resolve to play it by ear? Did they know the Hoyts were having a family dinner that Sunday? Had they heard from Kay that all the dinner guests had gone home?

Harold Nokes stated in his confession that he and Ena had gone out to eat on Sunday evening and then drove to Culbertson to see his parents. Finding the senior Nokeses' home to be dark, they drove on to the Hoyt home. They did not return to McCook before going to the Hoyts. Thus, Harold would have had the gun with him as they ate dinner and as they drove to his parent's home. Though Harold Nokes was adamant that they went to Culbertson first to see his parents and then and only then went on to the Hoyt farm, the story about going to see his parents sounds false, because he had already seen his parents at a family dinner that noon. His story is inherently unbelievable, but it was his story.

As Harold detailed in his confession, he and Ena did not reach the Hoyt home until after 9:00 p.m. The Hoyts invited them in, although the Nokeses had not given them any advance notice of the visit. Harold asked the Hoyts to return with them to the Nokeses' home in McCook. He suggested that they could then call Kay and ask her to join them, so that they could discuss the situation and hopefully arrive at an understanding. The Hoyts accepted the invitation, though no one called Kay from her parents' house to see if she was at home.

In fact, Kay *was* at home. She had engaged a babysitter, who arrived at 6:30 p.m. Kay, who said she was waiting for a phone call, remained at home. At 9:30, though she had not yet received a call, Kay dismissed the sitter. When questioned later by Lieutenant Grieb of the patrol as to why she had engaged a babysitter but then stayed home, Kay was extremely evasive. No definitive reason has ever surfaced.

According to Harold Nokes, he drove the Hoyts to McCook in his car so that they might discuss matters further on the drive. Ena Nokes followed, driving the Hoyts' car. Why Mrs. Hoyt did not drive Ena Nokes in the Hoyt car has never been satisfactorily answered. During the trip to McCook, Edwin Hoyt became agitated and accused Harold of being a liar and of blackmailing Kay. When they reached the Nokeses' home, Harold Nokes parked his car in the driveway, and Ena pulled the Hoyt car into the driveway behind them.

Located in a lower-middle-class neighborhood, the Nokeses' one-story home was small, with two bedrooms. The lots were not spacious, no more than fifty feet in width, providing little space between homes. Harold suggested that they all go down to the basement so that the neighbors would not hear if voices were raised.

The Nokeses' basement had three rooms: a family room, a laundry room, and a bedroom. The basement stairs led from the kitchen down into the family room. The door to the laundry room was next to the stairs, while the bedroom was farthest from the stairs.

Edwin Hoyt was the first person down the stairs, and he entered the laundry room, motioning to Harold Nokes to follow. The two women remained in the family room, unable to see into the laundry room.

The laundry room had a washer, dryer, and sink along one wall and a freezer along the opposite wall. Edwin removed his glasses and placed them on the washer. Then, turning toward Harold, he said he had had enough of Harold's lies. The men were about twelve feet apart when Edwin cocked his right fist and began to move toward Harold. When Edwin was about three feet away, Harold pulled the pistol from his belt with his left hand and, without saying a word or giving Edwin any warning, shot him in the chest.

Hearing the shot, Wilma screamed, "Why didn't you kill Kay?" and ran toward the steps. As she reached the second step, Harold stepped out of the laundry room and shot her. She fell backward into a crumpled heap at the foot of the stairs.

The details of the killings are taken from Harold Nokes's court-reported confession, which he related to prosecutors in January 1974. During the confession, he was asked if Edwin Hoyt knew he had a gun on him that night or if Edwin had seen Harold Nokes draw the gun. Harold replied that he did not know. But it is quite significant that Harold Nokes said nothing to Edwin Hoyt. He did not tell Edwin to stop, did not warn him that he had a gun, did nothing but point, shoot, and kill.

Wilma Hoyt's cry, "Why didn't you kill Kay?" is very intriguing. If, as Harold Nokes related it, she and Ena Nokes were outside in the family room that made up most of the basement, why did she immediately assume her husband was dead? What was the meaning of her remark about her daughter? Why did she try to flee, instead of entering the laundry room to check on her husband?

After the shootings, Ena Nokes ran upstairs to see if the noise had alerted the neighbors. When she returned, she told Harold that two of their neighbors who had been out on their porch with the porch light on had turned it out and gone inside.

Harold then urged his wife to leave and told her he would call the police after she was gone. Ena, however, refused to go. Harold stated in his confession that after this conversation, he examined the Hoyts to make sure they were dead. They were. Harold then went upstairs to the bathroom and vomited.

When he had purged his stomach, if not his conscience, he returned to the basement, where he and his wife discussed their dilemma. Something had to be done with the bodies, or the authorities had to be summoned. Ena reminded Harold that they had to think about their two children, and Harold realized that he had to conceal his actions or face prosecution. The discovery of the bodies would, for all practical purposes, mean the end of life as they knew it. One or both of them might well go to prison for life or face the death penalty.

Harold's most pressing problem was that his shoulder was so weak that he could not carry the bodies up the basement stairs. Though surely he and Ena could together have dragged the bodies upstairs, Harold decided instead that his only course of action was to cut up the bodies into manageable parts. Ena's role in making this decision is unknown, but it is a virtual certainty that they together discussed all of the processes and consequences of disposal. They were both experienced in field dressing game. Indeed, on the evening when Sawdon and a patrol officer questioned Ena about the affair, the men spent a long time questioning her about her hunting prowess and led her through a detailed step-by-step recitation of her experience shooting and field dressing a deer.

No one is certain as to the time at which the Nokeses reached this decision, but it must have been around midnight. The Nokeses had not arrived at the Hoyt farm until after 9:00 p.m., and the parties had talked there before leaving for McCook. The drive to town from Culbertson would have taken twenty-five to thirty minutes; although the murders took place almost as soon as the parties reached the Nokeses' house, an hour or two elapsed while Harold and Ena tried to decide on a course of action.

Before Harold began his macabre work, Ena drove the Hoyts' car from the Nokeses' home to St. Catherine's Hospital, where she parked it on the street. Harold picked her up in their car, and they returned home to begin the rest of their night's work.

The laundry room was turned into an abattoir. Harold sent Ena upstairs during the butchery, telling her he didn't want her to be involved, but she soon returned to assist. Harold began by dismembering the body of Edwin Hoyt, using a butcher knife and an ax that he kept in his state-furnished pickup. The butcher knife had a wooden handle and an eight- or nine-inch blade, which he sharpened two or three times during the course of his evening's work.

Gripping the ax halfway up the handle with his left hand, Harold used the instrument to break some of Edwin Hoyt's bones, remove the limbs, and then sever the head. Harold then used the knife to slice the torso in half vertically and into thirds horizontally. Blood flowed over the washroom floor as the dismemberment advanced. During the butchering process, the .22-caliber bullet fell out of the torso onto the floor. Harold recovered it and later threw it away when he disposed of the viscera. As he cut the body into manageable sizes using the butcher knife, while also cutting away the clothing, he and Ena wrapped the severed parts in freezer paper left over from fall hunting trips, sealing the packages with masking tape.

After finishing with the dissection and packaging of Edwin Hoyt's body, Harold turned to the corpse of Wilma Hoyt, which was still lying where it had fallen at the foot of the stairs. During all their trips up and down the stairs, the Nokeses had been stepping over her prostrate remains.

Harold Nokes dragged Mrs. Hoyt's body into the laundry room by the arm and repeated the butchering process. The bullet that had killed her had not completely penetrated her body and was protruding from her skin. Harold seized it and threw it away with the bullet that had killed Edwin. He did not, however, remove any of Wilma Hoyt's rings, an oversight that would spell disaster to his hopes of concealing his crime.

After the bodies were both dismembered and wrapped, the Nokeses stored the packages in their freezer. There was some meat already in the freezer, so Harold removed it, placed the body parts in the bottom of the freezer, then placed the meat back on top.

After the packages containing the body parts had been stored, Harold turned his attention to the visceral organs, which he had placed in a large plastic trash can. He took the trash can and drove approximately seventeen miles west of McCook, where he dumped the contents in a deep ravine, accessible from the highway, near a monument memorializing the Massacre Canyon slaying of a Pawnee band by the Sioux. He then drove home, taking the trash can with him. The trip was made in the early morning hours. And no neighbor appears to have noticed the activity, or at least none commented on it when questioned by the police.

When Harold returned home, Ena was still in the process of cleaning the basement. She used a hose to scrub the laundry room floor and cleaned the floor where Mrs. Hoyt's blood had spilled at the foot of the stairs. Harold did not state in his confession if Ena had made a trip outside to retrieve the hose and drag it down the stairs. Such late night activity might well have alerted any but the soundest-sleeping neighbors. But nothing was reported by the neighbors to the police, nor did anyone comment on it when the police and patrol questioned the neighbors.

The following day, Harold Nokes paid a visit to the Walkers, his next-door neighbors, and told them that his father was very ill in Culbertson. Harold explained that if they heard cars coming and going in the middle of the night, it was because the Nokeses were responding to calls for assistance at the parents' home. The ploy must have worked, as the Walkers were very noncommittal when questioned by law enforcement officers concerning the events of September 23.

As part of the cleanup, Harold gathered a bloody rug that had been at the foot of the basement stairs, all of the Hoyts' clothing, and the clothes he and Ena had been wearing and packed them in a cardboard box. Then he and Ena both went to work, as it was almost 8:00 a.m. Harold made it on time, but Ena was a few minutes late to her post at East Ward Elementary School.

Harold Nokes was a foreman for the State of Nebraska Department of Roads; when he got to work on the morning of September 24, he sent a detachment of his men to Culbertson to start a fire in the highway-department equipment yard to burn rotted guardrail posts. Harold then returned home about 9:00 a.m. He placed the cardboard box containing the bloodied clothes, shoes, and Wilma's purse in his pickup and drove to Trenton, west of McCook. He threw the Hoyts' glasses and Edwin Hoyt's billfold into Trenton Lake, also known as Swanson Reservoir, and then returned to Culbertson. He sent the workers who were tending the fire to a job at Benkleman, a small town west of Trenton. While he was alone, he retrieved the box and its gruesome contents from the pickup and threw it into the fire. He stayed in Culbertson, watching the fire until about 2:30 in the afternoon, when he returned to McCook, tossing the bloody ax into Frenchman Creek on his way home.

After arriving home, Harold Nokes sent Ena to buy some additional plastic trash cans at a McCook store. As dusk settled, the Nokeses packed the containers of body parts into the plastic trash cans and placed the cans in the trunk of their car. They did not have enough cans to hold all of the grisly packages, so they placed the excess in their boat. They hitched the boat to their car and set out eastward for Harry Strunk Lake in Frontier County. It was raining as they drove away, which raised the eyebrows of people watching them leave. Had the Walkers seen them leave in their boat in the rain, they might have wondered why the Nokeses were not staying home in case Harold's father needed their help.

Upon reaching the lake, the Nokeses loaded all the body parts into their boat and launched it, checking all the while to see if any other people were in the area. When they reached the middle of the lake, they unwrapped the packages of frozen flesh and hurled the body parts into the lake, along with the knife used in the butchery. While the Nokeses were engaged in their ghastly dumping, a few small body parts did not submerge but floated on the surface of the lake. They returned to shore, took the boat out of the water, built a fire, and burned the blood-soaked freezer paper that had contained the parts. Harold concealed the body parts that had not submerged in a mud bank near the fire. The Nokeses then returned to their home in McCook.

The following Saturday, September 29, Harold and Ena went back to the lake to see if any of the parts they had thrown overboard had surfaced. Why they waited almost a week to do so is a mystery. Ena stayed in the car while Harold reconnoitered the area. They did not take the boat, so his surveillance was done on foot. He found seven or eight small pieces of flesh that had washed up on the rocks that covered the dam, and he placed a large rock on top of them. The Nokeses then left the lake and did not return.

5

The Powwow

Kay Hein attempted to call her parents several times on Monday, September 24, but had no success in reaching them. Kay called Jerry Meyers, one of the Hoyts' neighbors, and asked if he would check the Hoyt farm. Mrs. Meyers soon reported back that no one was home, the Hoyts' car was gone, the house was locked, and the bedroom window was open. It had rained an inch and a half early Monday morning in the area of the Hoyt farm. Because the farmyard was not paved, any traffic would have left tracks on the wet earth, but there were no car tracks in the yard. Kay then called her sister, Donna Elmer, with her concerns. Donna, a novice pilot, went to McCook on Tuesday and, in company with her flight instructor, flew over the Hoyt farm to see if the car might be in one of the pastures. Nothing was visible. After the flight, Donna picked up Kay, and the two of them drove to the farm. Kay knew where a key had been hidden, and they inspected the house.

They found the pan in which the ham had been cooked on Sunday still soaking in the sink and ten dollars in cash lying on top of the television set. Two plates with cantaloupe rinds were in the living room. The Hoyts' night wear was laid out on the pillows of their bed, but the bed had not been slept in. The only signs of activity in the yard were the tracks left by the car of Mrs. Meyer when she had performed Kay's requested inspection. Neither Mr. Hoyt's billfold nor Mrs. Hoyt's purse were to be found, though Mrs. Hoyt's arthritis medicine was in its usual place.

According to Donna Elmer, Kay was very nervous throughout the search and kept repeating that she knew something awful had happened to their parents. She asked Donna to look under beds, in the barn, in the shop—all places no one would think to look. If she knew that Harold Nokes had gone to see her parents and that he had failed to call when her parents were at his home, she must have been very concerned.

Because she was the only family member living in McCook, Kay's home became a place during the investigation where the family gathered to exchange information. The Elmers drove from their home in Indianola every day, and as more Hoyt family members arrived in McCook, they filled Kay's small white bungalow almost to overflowing. After several family meetings on Tuesday, when all the family in the area had gathered at Kay's house, Larry Hoyt, a nephew of Edwin and Wilma, called a Lincoln attorney with whom he had done business and requested the name of a private investigator. The attorney recommended Robert Sawdon.

A World War II hero, wounded and decorated in the fighting in Normandy immediately after D-day, Sawdon had been an outstanding detective on the Lincoln police force for years. He had recently retired and opened an office as a private detective. He was a master of interrogation and well acquainted with law enforcement personnel all across Nebraska. The Hoyt family contacted Sawdon, who agreed to come to McCook on Monday, October 1. He was engaged at a rate of $150.00 for an eight hour day, plus expenses.

The family had already notified the state patrol and the Red Willow County Sheriff's Office that Edwin and Wilma Hoyt were missing. Both offices had replied that since there was no evidence that a crime had been committed, there was little they could do. The McCook patrol office notified the sheriff of Hitchcock County, where Culbertson is located; the sheriff went to the Hoyt farm and looked around but found nothing suspicious, nothing warranting an investigation.

On Wednesday, September 26, Owen Elmer and Larry Hoyt flew over the area searching for the Hoyts' car. A search undertaken on the ground by Kay, Donna, Larry Hoyt's wife, and several neighbors turned up nothing. The family notified the Kansas and Colorado state patrols and contacted local radio and TV media outlets with information about the Hoyts' disappearance.

On Thursday a relative spotted the Hoyt car parked at the hospital. The police were notified, and on that the same day, Jack Sexton of the patrol arrived from North Platte to inspect and inventory the car. The car was locked. There were no keys. The windows were up. There was no sign of mud on the car, which meant it had not been moved since Sunday night or Monday morning, when it had rained. The car was parked on the east side of the hospital, directly in front of the entrance.

Sexton used a skeleton key to open the car and dusted the rearview mirror and glove compartment for fingerprints. A patrolman removed samples of dirt and grass from the frame and bumper. They inventoried the contents of the car, and Sexton noticed that the front seat was quite close to the steering wheel, indicating that the car had been driven by a short person. Ena Nokes is five feet tall, while all the Hoyts were substantially taller than Ena.

On Friday, Herb Hoyt arrived from his naval base in South Carolina, and family and neighbors continued to comb the area through the weekend. On Sunday, September 30, Donna and Owen Elmer, Kay and Herb Hoyt and Jerry Anne Hoyt

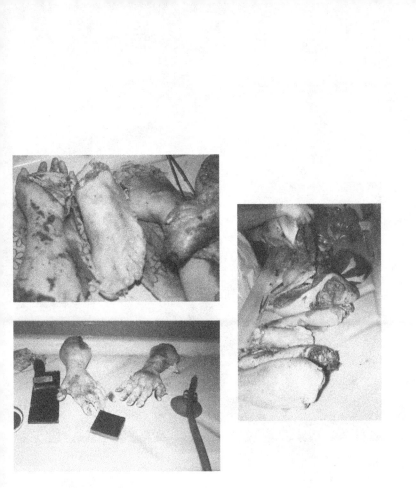

1-3. Body parts recovered from Strunk Lake in Cambridge Mortuary.
Courtesy of Lannie Roblee.

4. Nokes home at 903 G Street, McCook, Nebraska.
Courtesy of author.

5. Kay Hein home at 127 West O Street, McCook, Nebraska.
Courtesy of author.

6. Area near Massacre Canyon. Courtesy of author.

7. Bob Sawdon as Lincoln police deputy chief.
Courtesy of Bob Sawdon Jr.

8. Sgt. Jack Sexton in state patrol uniform. Courtesy of Pat Sexton.

9. Lannie Roblee in 2014. Courtesy of Lannie Roblee.

In Memorium

Wilma and Edwin Hoyt

10. Funeral program of Wilma and Edwin Hoyt.
Courtesy of Owen Elmer.

GARY EUGENE HOWELL
College Prep: M Club 1, 2, 3, 4; FFA 1, 2; Track 1, 2, Lettered 1, 2, Student Librarian 1.

LEON KLINTON HOYT
"Speed"
College Prep: M Club 3, 4; Thespians 3, 4, Pep Band 2, 3, 4, Dance Band 4, Band 1, 2, 3, 4, Football 3, 4, Lettered 3, 4, Junior Class Play 3.

KAY LOUISE HOYT
Commercial: Pep Club 2, 3, 4; Thespians 3, 4, Treasurer 4; Band 1, 2, 3, 4, Pep Band 2, 3, 4, Letter 3, 4, FHA 2, 3; Student Secretary 4, Junior Class Play 3, Senior Class Play 4, A.U.M. 3, 4.

ROBERT BURKE HOYT
"Mighty Mouse"
College Prep and Agriculture: FFA 2, 3, 4, County Government 3, Student Librarian 2.

CLASS OF '61

RONALD JAY HUET
"Huey"
General

JOYCELYN HUET
"Joyce"
General: Pep Club 2, 3; FHA 2.

DIANE TRUDA KEENE
"Di"
College Prep: Pep Club 2, 3, 4, Thespians 4; Band 1, 2, 3, 4, Pep Band 2, 3, 4, Lettered 1, 2, 3, 4, Dance Band 3, 4, Small Ensembles 1, 2.

BEVERLY ANN JOHNETTE
"Bev"
College Prep: Yearbook Staff 4; Band 2, 3, Pep Band 3, Lettered 3; FHA 3, 4.

THEDA BETH JONES
"Beth"
Home Economics: Les Chanteurs 2; FHA 3, 4.

WILLIAM FRANK HUNTER
"Bill"
College Prep: Math Club 3, 4; Thespians 3, 4; Band 1, 2, 3, 4, Pep Band 3, 4, State Clinic 4, Junior Class Play.

11. Kay Hoyt as high school senior in 1961 McCook High annual.
Courtesy of McCook Senior High.

12. Ena and Harold Nokes leaving McCook for prison. Note Harold's chains. UPI telephoto.

returned to the farm to determine what the Hoyts might have been wearing at the time of their disappearance. They found $225 in traveler's checks and the Hoyt's passports, but they were unable to decide how the Hoyts were dressed.

Owen Elmer had acted as chairman of the family gatherings during the first few meetings but began to feel that the scope of the problem was beyond his capabilities. He contacted Edwin Hoyt's brother, Thurber, who had been a high-ranking military officer, and urged him to come to McCook to direct the family's efforts. Thurber, a retired air force colonel, agreed to do so.

Thurber arrived from his home in California during the first week and assumed command of the family efforts. During the family discussions, word about Kay's involvement with the Nokeses and Edwin Hoyt's suspicions of possible blackmail were brought to everyone's attention by Whitey and Jerry Ann Hoyt, who had learned of it from Wilma. The family concluded that the Nokeses may have had something to do with the disappearances.

Adding to the family's suspicions was Kay's increasingly unsettled and agitated behavior. After Whitey and Jerry Anne arrived in McCook, a family member gave Jerry Anne a large plastic bag full of pills and told her not to let Kay have access to them under any circumstances, as she might try to commit suicide. The pills were Kay's, but no one remembers how they were discovered, or by whom, or why family members feared a suicide attempt. Whitey and his family stayed at Kay's house, and Jerry Ann later recalled to the author that her behavior during their stay was bizarre. One night, Kay woke her girls in the middle of the night to move them from their bedroom to another; after a short time, she repeated the process, moving them back to the original bedroom. She offered no explanation for her behavior.

On Friday the twenty-eighth, Sergeant Sexton returned to McCook from North Platte and interviewed Kay Hein, Donna Elmer, Owen Elmer, Larry Hoyt, Roger Hoyt, and Herbert Hoyt. Sexton was aware of the sign investigation previously conducted by Tumblin of the patrol and Deputy Haegen. Kay repeated the information she had told Tumblin during her discussion with Sexton and told him that she thought that either Harold or another of her sexual partners could be responsible for her parents' disappearance. Harold, however, was her top suspect.

That Kay fingered Harold in the disappearance of her parents was something new, since she had not placed the blame for the graffiti on him. She told Sexton that she felt that her parents' disappearance was her fault because of her involvement with Harold. She believed that someone, probably Harold Nokes, had called her parents with a story that an illness or injury had befallen Kay or one of her daughters, thereby convincing the Hoyts to drive to the hospital. Kay felt sure her parents had been kidnapped upon their arrival in McCook. This may well have been exactly what happened. But it does not explain the unusual position of the seat in the car.

Robert Sawdon, the private investigator from Lincoln, arrived in McCook on Monday, October 1, driving a Jaguar, wearing a trench coat, and looking for all the world like TV detective Peter Falk as Columbo. He booked a room at the Cedar Inn, a quiet establishment on the east edge of McCook.

Sawdon met with the family on October 1, after he had met with the patrol and learned of the Tumblin sign investigation. He asked extensive questions concerning the family's ideas as to what had happened to the Hoyts and why. Kay's sexual involvement, and Harold Nokes's role as the object of her affections, served as the main topic of the discussion. For some of the family, their conferences and Sawdon's questions were their first inkling of Kay's promiscuity. The information must have been an eye-opener to the extended members of the family. After the family meeting adjourned, Sawdon visited both the Red Willow County sheriff and the McCook chief of police and solicited their views as to what had transpired.

On Tuesday, October 2, Sawdon spoke to Sexton and others at the patrol office. The patrol was still viewing the disappearances as a missing persons matter, as there was no evidence that a crime had been committed. Sawdon asked that the patrol contact Harold Nokes and ask him to come to the patrol office. They complied, and some fifteen minutes later Harold Nokes arrived at the office.

Harold Nokes and Sawdon had an extensive conversation, with Sawdon doing the questioning. Though Sawdon used a tape recorder, the first portion of the interview was not recorded. In the second half of the interview, Harold admitted that he had had an affair with Kay, though he insisted it was over. He admitted that Ena might have suspected the affair but maintained that he had not told her about it.

The failure to record the first portion of the discussion may have been deliberate. No one knows whether Sawdon tried to convey to Harold Nokes that he was acting in a law enforcement capacity. Certainly one acting under color of the law would have a great deal more coercive power in eliciting information than a private detective asking questions. If Harold Nokes was thinking clearly, he would have felt no responsibility to talk to someone who was not a law enforcement officer.

The graffiti accusing Kay of promiscuity formed a major part of the questioning. Harold said he had scrubbed a number of messages off bridges and road signs and denied having written any of them. Sawdon asked Nokes if he had any guns, including rifles, shotguns, or handguns. Nokes replied that his shoulder was in such bad shape that he could no longer fire a rifle or a shotgun, so he had recently purchased a .22-caliber pistol to use for small game and target shooting.

Sawdon pressed Nokes repeatedly to take a polygraph test, using a variety of stratagems, but Nokes refused every time the question was put to him. The interview finally terminated after almost two hours, with Sawdon advising Nokes that he would want to talk to him again.

On Wednesday, October 3, Sawdon met again with the Hoyt family and then interviewed two of Kay's sexual partners, both of whom ultimately confessed their involvement with her after an initial denial. One of the two, in fact, confessed to more trysts with Kay than she had acknowledged to the state patrol. Sawdon was a persistent and skillful interrogator, but it is hard to imagine why either man confessed to Sawdon, unless he was accompanied by a law enforcement officer. That, however, is doubtful, since it wasn't until later that day that the body parts were discovered at Strunk Lake. Around 4:00 p.m., the patrol notified Sawdon of the discovery, and he proceeded to the lake, where he met with Sheriff Lannie Roblee of Frontier County and Sergeant Divis of the patrol.

Lannie Roblee was appointed to be the sheriff of Frontier County in 1970, when he was twenty-five years old. Previously he had been a policeman in Lexington for four years, working the night shift while attending Kearney State College (now the University of Nebraska–Kearney) during the day. The sheriff in Frontier County had died, and Roblee applied and was chosen as his successor. He subsequently was elected six times to four-year terms before retiring in 1995.

Roblee today is genial, intelligent, and witty. His receding hair is closely cropped, and he gives the impression of significant physical strength. His frame carries more weight than it did when he was a young and eager law enforcer, but he is obviously a man of energy and vitality even today at sixty-four.

When Roblee became sheriff, every town in Frontier County had a town marshal or a town constable. Roblee worked out a deal with the Nebraska Crime Commission whereby the sheriff (Roblee) would furnish services to all of the county's towns, and the towns would pay the sheriff for doing so. The sheriff and his deputies thus patrolled the highways and byways of the county.

In the three years that he had served as sheriff prior to the Hoyt murders, Roblee had not been involved in investigating any major criminal activity. Like most sheriffs in rural Nebraska counties, Roblee served papers, arrested speeders, and dealt with minor violations of the law. But the young sheriff was bright, enthusiastic, and well equipped to deal with a sensational murder in his territory.

Roblee took charge of the activity at the lake, as the various law enforcement personnel searched the area and discovered additional body parts. He was also present that evening when Donna Elmer was shown the rings that had been on the hand found at the lake. When Donna identified the rings as her mother's, the missing persons case became a murder investigation.

The morning following the discovery of the bodies, October 4, Sawdon visited Frontier County attorney Fred Schroeder at his office in Curtis, at Schroeder's request. Schroeder told Sawdon that Paul Douglas, the Lancaster County attorney in Lincoln and a veteran prosecutor, had recommended Sawdon as a capable investigator, one who could assist Frontier County sheriff Lannie Roblee. Douglas and Schroeder had been classmates at the University of Nebraska's Law College, and Schroeder relied on Douglas's expertise in handling criminal matters throughout the course of the investigation. Douglas knew Sawdon very well, as Douglas was the chief prosecutor of all the criminals tried in state court in Lincoln, many of whom had been nabbed by Sawdon, who was head of the Criminal Division at the Lincoln Police Department at the time. Schroeder and Sawdon reached a contractual accord whereby Frontier County would pay Sawdon to act as a consultant to Sheriff Roblee and the patrol during the investigation. Sawdon returned to Lincoln to wrap up pending matters before returning to McCook the following week.

While Sawdon was in Lincoln, the patrol, no doubt red faced about its earlier lethargy in the case, continued the investigation. For experienced technical assistance, they brought in several of their heavy hitters, one of whom was Lt. Donald Grieb from North Platte, who headed up the patrol's criminal investigations in western Nebraska.

Grieb interviewed a number of the Nokeses' neighbors about activity at the Nokeses' home. The neighbors were generally reticent, but several did tell the patrol that Harold Nokes took his boat out on the rainy evening of September 24. Many people in McCook also came forward voluntarily with information, an amalgam of rumor and misinformation. One beauty shop operator told police that Wilma Hoyt had called for a hair appointment on Monday, the day after the killings. The investigation did little to calm the fears of McCook residents. Many young mothers refused to allow their offspring to go trick-or-treating on Halloween.

Sawdon returned to McCook on October 8 and met with Sheriff Roblee and all the patrol investigators. They exchanged information and began an extensive round of questioning of family and neighbors.

On October 9 Lieutenant Grieb interrogated Harold Nokes

for a second time. Harold again acknowledged that he and Kay had carried on an affair for some two years. This time, however, he admitted that he had told Ena of the affair and said that she had forgiven him. Grieb had interviewed Kay earlier that day, and she had admitted her sexual activity with Harold but said nothing about Ena's involvement.

Sawdon continued his work of interview and analysis; on Thursday, October 11, acting on a hunch that Kay Hein had not told everything about her involvement with Harold Nokes, Sawdon went to her home and vigorously interrogated her at length. Finally, Kay acknowledged her sexual activity with both Harold and Ena and furnished all the prurient details of time, place, and position. Sawdon then took her to the patrol office that afternoon, where she repeated her story so that it could be recorded and transcribed.

Once they had heard Kay's tale, patrol officers determined that Harold and Ena Nokes must be requestioned. They picked the two up at their home and brought them to the patrol office. Grieb talked to Harold, while another officer and Sawdon confronted Ena. Both Kay and Harold freely admitted the ménage à trois. Ena never did. Whether the patrol advised Harold and Ena that they were suspects has never been made clear. They had not been arrested at the time and may not have been given Miranda warnings.

Grieb had expected Harold would acknowledge the ménage à trois in Ena's presence. When he did not, Grieb sent Sawdon and Ena out of the room and resumed his questioning of Harold.

After everyone but Harold and Grieb had left the room, Grieb asked Nokes if he had used his boat to take the Hoyt bodies to Strunk Lake. Nokes said he thought he should call an attorney. Grieb asked him if Ena had shot the Hoyts. Nokes denied it. Grieb then asked Harold if he had shot the

Hoyts, and he said no. Harold stated that his wife was not involved in the Hoyt's death or dismemberment in any way but refused to answer Grieb's further questions about his or Kay's involvement.

Harold Nokes then asked again if he could call his attorney, and Grieb showed him one of the patrol's phones. Harold said it was not located where he could have a private conversation. Though Grieb told him that he would step away, Nokes refused to use it. Nokes then asked Grieb why they thought he had taken the body parts to the lake and was told what the patrol had learned of his mysterious use of the boat on the evening of September 24.

For almost two more hours, Harold questioned Grieb about aspects of murder and penalties, while Grieb pressed for more information about Harold's involvement in the murders. Nokes continued to deny killing the Hoyts, but he neither admitted nor denied involvement in the disposal of the bodies, remaining silent when Grieb questioned him on this subject. Harold also continued to deny that Ena was involved in any way. Given how much information Harold Nokes was offering, it's unclear whether he was distraught or just stupid. The cardinal rule, even without advice from a lawyer, is "keep your mouth shut." Almost everyone knows that. Not everyone follows it.

Finally, Nokes asked again about contacting an attorney and this time used the phone. When he failed to reach an attorney in Minden whom he called, Harold called his son in Lincoln, where the son was in school, and asked him to secure an attorney for him.

After the call, the patrol arrested both Harold and Ena Nokes, locking them in separate cells at the McCook jail. The next morning, Richard Hove, Kearney attorney and former Minden resident, arrived at the jail to act as the attorney for the Nokeses. Hove had been secured by the Nokeses' son, Al, who knew Hove because they were both members of the National Guard. Hove was capable, outgoing, and self-confident, with over a decade's experience in trial work and criminal defense. He told Frontier County attorney Schroeder that the police didn't have enough evidence to hold the Nokeses in jail. Schroeder agreed. The two lawyers considered sending them to the state hospital in Lincoln as a form of protective custody while the investigation continued, but the hospital refused to accept them. Hove and Schroeder instead asked the Nokeses to stay with their daughter in Ord, Nebraska, for a few days, which they did.

That Hove was willing to have the Nokeses taken into any form of protective custody is surprising. There was no evidence that they had committed any crime. Harold Nokes's disjointed babbling to Grieb about the shooting and the disposal of the bodies would not withstand a motion to release them on a writ of habeas corpus. A search warrant had not yet been issued, and even if it had been, there was no reason for the Nokeses to be held while their house was searched.

The *McCook Gazette*, the *Lincoln Journal*, and the *Lincoln Star* were all following the story closely. Anxious that the media not release the names of his clients, Hove called a press conference, addressing the assembled reporters in McCook. Hove admonished the press not to report that his clients had been arrested or to give their names and hinted at legal action if the Nokeses were identified.

The papers made no attempt to interview the Hoyt family or the Nokeses. Apparently Hove's warning had sufficed. The *Gazette* continued to give the murders front-page treatment, and its sensational stories kept McCook in a furor. On October 12 the *Gazette* headlined, "McCook Man, Wife Held for Questioning," but provided no names. On October 16 a front-page banner proclaimed, "McCook Man, Wife in Private Custody," but again, no names were published. Despite this lack of details, circulation of the *McCook Gazette* soared to new heights as readers eagerly sought the latest news, much of which was pure speculation. The Lincoln and Omaha papers were more circumspect, usually confining their coverage to wire service reports on an inside page.

Though the papers dutifully danced around the question of identity, they reported that a warrant had been issued by the Red Willow County Court on October 12 to search the residence of Mr. and Mrs. Harold Nokes at 903 Avenue G in McCook. The issuance of the warrant and the location of the search were public records that the papers were free to report. Why authorities sought the warrant and why it was issued were not made clear. There was no evidence of any activity at the Nokeses' home, and the only evidence of weapons being used against the Hoyts was the body fragment containing what appeared to be a bullet hole. Judge Cloyd Clark of Red Willow County issued the search warrant for the Nokeses' home, following a hearing at which Grieb testified. No record was made of the testimony. It could not have been compelling if true. Clark was a fledgling on the bench when the warrant came before him. There were two McCook judges in the county court district that encompassed southwestern Nebraska. Wendell Cheney handled matters in Red Willow County, including McCook, while Clark generally handled all the other counties in the district. Cheney, however, wanted nothing to do with the case, so Clark heard it essentially by default. Cheney had known Harold Nokes's father and Ena Nokes for years because of their service in the county courthouse. After the Nokeses had been convicted and prior to their sentencing, Cheney even wrote a letter on their behalf to the probation officer conducting the presentence investigation.

The warrant hearing took place in the late afternoon. Hove was apparently anxious to get out of town and return to his home and law practice in Kearney, because he did not vigorously contest the issuance of the warrant. Grieb testified about the alleged ménage à trois and the Nokeses' trip with their boat to the lake. Clark acknowledged to the author in an interview that he believed probable cause existed to issue the warrant because of the sexual involvement of Kay and the Nokeses.

When Harold Nokes ultimately filed an appeal with the Nebraska Supreme Court, one of the more interesting contentions in the appeal was that there was no probable cause for the issuance of the search warrant. That issue was not decided by the supreme court, which decided the case on the rule that a guilty plea waives any defects. But as to the issuance of the search warrant, the patrol was not searching for evidence of adulterous sex—it was looking for evidence of who killed the Hoyts. And there was nothing concrete to connect the Nokeses to that crime.

The search of the Nokeses' home was carried out on October 12 by a number of law enforcement personnel from the patrol, McCook police, and Roblee's office. The investigators inventoried the house; removed some clothing found in the basement, including a blood-stained night gown (it was later ascertained that the blood was menstrual blood); took samples of what appeared to be blood from the floor drain in the basement laundry room; and jackhammered a few bits of concrete from the floor of the laundry room. They also inventoried the contents of the Nokeses' car before the Nokeses left for their daughter's home in Ord.

The patrol sent the blood taken from the floor drain to the state laboratory for analysis, and the lab determined it was animal blood. Nothing found in the search was in any way related to the Hoyts or to their blood types. Ena Nokes's cleaning job had been thorough and successful, but she had had many days since September 23 to remove any evidence. Her cleaning job on the night of the murders was no doubt effective, but she surely supplemented it with later efforts. However, why the drain yielded traces of animal blood, no doubt left there from wild game the Nokeses had processed before the murders occurred, but no trace of the Hoyts' blood is hard to understand. The investigators were stymied.

Bits, pieces, and snippets of information continued to be amassed by the investigators over the course of several days. Law enforcement discovered that on Tuesday, October 2, Harold Nokes had taken his boat to a shop in McCook for repairs. His justification, given to anyone who had asked, for taking his boat out on the evening of September 24 was that the engine was not working properly and he wanted to test it in order to explain the problem to the repairman. The repairman tested the engine and performed minor repairs to the carburetor. So as early as October 2, Harold Nokes was at least thinking about establishing an alibi, even though he had not yet been questioned by Sawdon, questioning that occurred later that day.

On October 12 Kay Hein gave Sawdon the dress, slip, and bra that Harold Nokes had ripped in half as she struggled to get away from him on the day she had been lured to their home by Ena's concocted story about cutting her hand. She also gave him the lightbulb destined for her front porch that had been painted red. The same day, before the Nokeses were released from jail in McCook, Harold told the sheriff of Red Willow County, "I belong in jail, but my wife doesn't." Apparently the sheriff did nothing to follow up on such an unusual statement. Harold must have been feeling Sawdon's hot breath on his back.

After the Nokeses left for Ord, Sawdon returned to Lincoln, where he met with Attorney General Clarence Meyer for legal guidance and Lancaster County attorney Paul Douglas, who had agreed to help Fred Schroeder whenever prosecution became necessary. On October 26 a strategy meeting was held in Douglas's office in Lincoln. Present were Douglas, Sawdon, Schroeder, Roblee, several officers of the patrol, and, toward the end of the meeting, Nebraska governor J. J. Exon. It was highly unusual for a governor to become involved in a criminal matter, but the sensational nature of the case, coupled with the fact that Exon, a former state chairman of the Nebraska Democratic Party, was well known in McCook, led to his attendance. The parties discussed methods of getting the Nokeses to confess. Schroeder reported that he had consulted a forensic psychiatrist in Denver, who had advised him that if the Nokeses were separated, they would lose their mutual support system and might well crack under the strain.

Another reason for Exon's attendance was his involvement in the fallout from the Fitzgibbons case. Earlier in October, Exon had called Tumblin to the Governor's Mansion in Lincoln and spent three hours questioning him at length about the Fitzgibbons case. The governor told Tumblin that Mayor Don Blank of McCook had contacted him, concerned that there had been a cover-up. The Fitzgibbons case no doubt heightened scrutiny of the McCook Police Department and the state patrol, giving Exon a vested interest in the investigation of the Hoyt murders.

Since the Nokeses now had a lawyer, investigators no longer had easy access to them. The patrol instead focused on interviewing neighbors and following up on rumors and false leads, including tales of marital infidelity that involved several other McCook citizens. The Nokeses' neighbors, however, were evasive and unwilling to become involved in the investigation. Virtually everyone the patrol contacted spoke well of Harold and Ena and refused to believe that they could have committed such a heinous crime. Opinions of Kay Hein, however, were not as gracious. A number of women told the patrol of Kay's promiscuity and paired her with a number of McCook males, both married and unmarried. None of the stories proved to be true. Kay's neighbors also related that someone had written "Hot Ass Bitch" on her house in July, and that they had attempted to remove the message, which seemed to be written in black crayon.

In a bizarre attempt to crack the Nokeses, Douglas and Schroeder found a woman in McCook who bore an uncanny resemblance to Wilma Hoyt. They dressed her in Mrs. Hoyt's clothing after seeking permission from the family and seated her next to Ena Nokes at the lunch counter of a McCook restaurant. Ena never batted an eye.

On November 5 a memorial service for the Hoyts was held in the Culbertson Methodist Church, the church that they had attended. The small building was packed to overflowing. All the body parts that had been recovered were placed in two caskets, which were present at the service, though they remained closed. Interment took place that day in the Hoyts' lot at Culbertson Cemetery.

On November 10 a team of divers from the Douglas County Sheriff's Office searched the surface of Strunk Lake unsuccessfully for additional body parts. On November 11 two of the divers searched underwater, but due to the turbid condition of the water, they were unable to discover anything of relevance.

Little progress was being made in building a case against the Nokeses, so on November 20 Fred Schroeder filed an application in the District Court of Frontier County, seeking permission to implant a bug, or listening device, in the Nokeses' home and in their car. The application asked for twenty-four-hour-a-day monitoring of the Nokeses' home for a period of thirty days. Such a procedure had only recently been enacted into law by the Nebraska legislature, and there was no judicial decision interpreting the law or precedent allowing such action. The bulk of legal maneuvering took place in Frontier County, because the bodies were discovered there. The proper venue would have been the county in which the murders took place, but this fact was not yet known. Fred Schroeder was willing to act as the attorney in the petition for the listening device, while Red Willow County attorney Clyde Starrett wanted nothing to do with the investigation.

Starrett had been involved in the Ida Fitzgibbons case earlier that year. Despite McCook chief of police William Green's conclusion that Fitzgibbons's death was a suicide, Starrett, as was his right under Nebraska statutes, proceeded with a six-man coroner's jury. The jury, called to determine if the death was a suicide or a homicide, met off and on over a period of some two weeks. They ultimately split three to three as to the cause of death.

Starrett's performance before the jury in the Fitzgibbons case was lackluster in the extreme. He presented neither Tumblin's nor Haegen's reports of their investigation of the case, nor were either of them called to testify. Starrett later explained that he was worried about the cost of the jury and that he disliked having businessmen subpoenaed for hours for their time for only a two-dollar-a-day reimbursement.

The hubbub surrounding the Fitzgibbons case, the public outcry, and the criticism of the McCook police made Clyde Starrett reluctant to become involved in another sensational case. He was only too happy to have someone else bear the laboring oar in the Hoyt murders.

The application to implant listening devices in the Nokeses' home and car was heard by Jack Hendrix, the district judge in McCook at the time of the murders. A dedicated Rotarian, Hendrix had no desire to publicly castigate community members who had engaged in illicit sexual activities. Later, when the Nokeses were sentenced and removed from the community, he sealed all the court records so that the identities of Kay's sexual partners would remain only rumors.

At the outset of the hearing, Schroeder was candid with the court. "We are at the point where it still appears that we do not have an adequate amount of information and evidence to file a first-degree murder charges [*sic*] and to obtain a conviction. . . . We doubt that the state has an adequate amount of evidence to prove their guilt beyond a reasonable doubt." Hendrix was concerned about Schroeder's admissions. He responded, "You are asking me to find probable cause when you feel that at this juncture you do not have sufficient evidence to file a prosecution case?" Schroeder bit the bullet and admitted that he had probable cause for filing murder charges but that he could not obtain a conviction on the present evidence. Hendrix must have swallowed hard but let him continue.

The hearing on the application began late in the afternoon of November 20 and continued on the following day. In support of the application, Lannie Roblee and Donald Grieb testified on the first day, and Kay Hein testified on the second. On the twenty-first, Judge Hendrix, in his court chambers, listened to two tapes of testimony by Kay Hein recorded by Richard Hove on November 17 in the presence of Lannie Roblee and Owen Elmer. The tapes related the details of Kay's affair with Harold and Ena Nokes. No one other than Roblee represented the state at the taping. Schroeder did not attend. Hendrix listened to the tapes from 10:35 a.m. to 2:15

74

p.m. Later that afternoon the hearing resumed, and Schroeder called Kay Hein as a witness. Kay's role at the hearing was to reinforce her statement on the tapes and earlier to Sawdon that Harold Nokes had threatened her, stating that "she would be sorry" when she terminated the affair. Since neither she nor the state had been represented by counsel at the time Hove questioned her, the probative value of the tapes was questionable, and her testimony on the twenty-first was necessary to support the taped conversation. Testifying under penalty of perjury, Kay reiterated, albeit briefly, the sexual threesome with Harold and Ena Nokes.

Kay had never listened to the tapes after having been questioned by Hove, so Schroeder was unable to have her authenticate them. At the urging of Judge Hendrix, Schroeder managed to secure from her the statement that everything she told Hove was true. No one knows how much influence the tapes had on Hendrix's ultimate decision to grant the application, but had Harold Nokes not confessed, a competent defense attorney attacking the probable cause for granting the bug could have placed any evidence gained by virtue of the bug in jeopardy.

Hendrix knew that Kay's testimony regarding Harold's statements was doubtful, as it was hearsay. He stated, "I think we should state here that the court recognizes that this is hearsay and will give this testimony only such credence as it determines in a hearing of this kind it should be given. And I make this statement so that we all understand what we are having here is hearsay testimony."

The Nebraska statutes authorizing a listening device required that there be probable cause that the persons to be bugged were guilty of the crime, in this case murder, specified in the application. Schroeder tried diligently over the course of the hearing to establish probable cause but never really did so. Perhaps Hendrix felt that, weak as the evidence was, if it would help catch a murderer, it was worth a try. Though Judge Hendrix was not anxious to break new legal ground by ordering the placement of the bug, he reluctantly approved the application.

At the conclusion of the hearing, Hendrix found that there was probable cause to believe that the Nokeses were guilty of murder. He also stated that all normal investigative procedures had been tried and had failed, a damning indictment of what had transpired thus far in the investigation.

Hendrix signed the order on November 21, and the investigators now faced the problem of gaining access to the Nokeses' house to install the listening device. The Nokeses had long since returned from Ord and were back at work. A member of the McCook office of the patrol was called on to open the house while Harold and Ena were at work. In test runs, he picked locks like a professional. But on the scene, with neighbors probably peeking from their windows, he proved so nervous that he was unable to unlock the door. A locksmith from Lincoln was brought out and quickly did the job. Bugging began on December 3. It is not clear whether the patrol or a deputy sheriff from Lincoln installed the bugs. Whoever performed the task did not do it well.

The installation of the bugs—one in a light in the living room, another in a bedroom light—allowed listeners, who included personnel from the patrol and the Frontier County Sheriff's Office, to hear conversations of the Nokeses. The bugs, however, ruined the reception of the Nokeses' television set. The eavesdroppers heard the Nokeses complain that they had no television reception, though the set had been working perfectly that morning. The Nokeses called a television repairman to fix the problem. Panicked, the listeners called the Red Willow County sheriff, who contacted the repairman to alert him that a bug had been installed in the house. He was told to fix the set without disturbing the listening device and was able to do so.

The interception of the Nokeses' conversations lasted for almost three weeks. No so-called "smoking gun," in which the Nokeses admitted the murder and discussed the disposal of the bodies, emerged. The listeners started in a motel room in downtown McCook, but because the reception there was not very good, they moved the listening and taping equipment to the basement of a state trooper's house about a block from the Nokeses' home. They used a master tape that was kept constantly running and additional equipment in the evenings, when they knew the Nokeses would be home. Lannie Roblee, who logged many hours as a listener, acknowledged that sometimes they captured intimate moments between the Nokeses but that the couple "were quiet about it." Sgt. Jack Sexton, who spent hours manning the taping equipment, said the Nokeses seldom said anything relevant except how much they disliked Sexton.

The Nokeses did discuss what might happen if they were arrested and charged with murder, and they resolved to commit suicide rather than face prison or the electric chair. They decided to carry codeine-based pills and to ingest them if arrested.

Lannie Roblee, a frequent and tireless listener, felt that the Nokeses were very careful about saying anything that would incriminate them. Ena and Harold, though, made what Roblee believed was one significant misstep. A week into the bugging, Harold commented to Ena, "We should have removed the rings." Roblee thought it likely that Harold was referring to the rings found on Wilma Hoyt's severed hand, a comment that showed an awareness of crucial evidence and one that could only have been known to the perpetrators. Some forty years later, Roblee was unable to recall the time or the other content of the conversation but was quite definite that Harold Nokes had made the comment.

The comment about the rings and the plan to commit suicide, along with the stalled investigation, galvanized Fred Schroeder to file first-degree murder charges against the Nokeses, and he did so in Frontier County in mid-December. Lannie Roblee arrested Harold and Ena in McCook on December 20. Harold was clearing snow off State Highways 6 and 34, which also constituted one of McCook's city streets, and Ena was arrested as she finished the day's work at school.

Harold was taken to the Frontier County jail in Curtis. He was the sole occupant. Because Curtis did not have facilities for female prisoners, Ena was taken to the Lincoln County jail in North Platte.

The reaction of the Hoyt family to the news of the arrests was one of relief, although they had not been told what evidence had been uncovered justifying the arrest. On December 20 the *McCook Gazette* devoted almost its entire front page to the story that Harold and Ena Nokes had been charged in the Hoyt murder. How the *Gazette* learned the story of the morning arrests in time to run a banner headline in its afternoon edition leads one to believe that Schroeder leaked to the paper before the arrests unfolded. After the *Gazette* had carried a front-page story on November 30 that there was no new progress in the Hoyt case, Schroeder contacted the paper and told them that "a new break was coming soon in the Hoyt case," as a front-page headline trumpeted on December 4. Again on December 6 the *Gazette* reported that "Charges Could Come Soon in Hoyt Case," and on December 17 the *Gazette* reported that Hoyt charges were expected "this week." These stories were no doubt based on Schroder's communications with the paper. Residents of McCook who knew the Nokeses found it hard to believe they were capable of murder or mutilation, but the general reaction of the town was one of relief that the perpetrators had been apprehended.

The Nokeses were now separated with no way to communicate with each other except through their lawyer. The time had arrived to test the theory of the Denver psychiatrist who had stated to Schroeder that one of the Nokeses would crack once they were separated.

6

The Pursuer

At the time of Harold Nokes's incarceration, the Frontier County jail in Curtis was located in the municipal office building, a low one-story structure that also housed the city clerk's office. The same building also contained an electrical generator that powered the Curtis city power plant. The generator was a noisy neighbor, and its revolutions and vibrations were not conducive to restful sleep for Harold Nokes, the sole occupant of the jail.

From his office, the sheriff could not see into the cells, which were behind him, but could hear any noise emanating from them. Each cell had a slot through which food could be passed, either by the sheriff or his deputies, without entering the cell.

Almost all the food for prisoners was purchased at a café directly across the street from the municipal building. The sheriff received a daily fee from the county for feeding the prisoners, a fee which usually exceeded the daily expenditures for food.

Because Roblee wanted Nokes to talk only to him, he was the only person who delivered food to Nokes's cell. The deputies checked on Harold at night, but the only real contact the inmate had was with Roblee.

Lannie Roblee had spent untold hours eavesdropping on the Nokeses after the bugs had been authorized and installed. He was aware of the Nokeses' plan to commit suicide, and so after Harold was arrested and jailed, Roblee searched Harold and his belongings carefully for any suicidal contraband. Roblee found tucked into the waistband of Nokes's civilian trousers a cellophane bag containing fifty-three codeine-laced pills. Roblee confiscated them and, the following day, informed the county judge handling Nokes's preliminary hearing at the courthouse in Stockville of the discovery.

Because Stockville, rather than Curtis, was the Frontier County seat, the county courthouse was in Stockville. Unique among Nebraska's courthouses, the tiny and antiquated courthouse in Stockville must have seemed like a trip back in time. For years, well into the second half of the twentieth century, the courthouse had no running water or indoor toilet facilities. Consequently, no women were called for jury duty in Frontier County. The town of Stockville was almost nonexistent. It had no restaurant. People in town for trials could eat at a church basement, where women of the congregation served food they had prepared, much like a covered-dish supper.

Ena had been taken to jail in North Platte, because Curtis had no facilities for female prisoners. Roblee's counterpart in North Platte, where Ena was incarcerated, discovered eighty-one pills in her brassiere and purse when she was checked in as a prisoner. Because the Nokeses were brought before the court in Stockville separately for their preliminary hearings, Harold was not aware that Ena's pills had been discovered.

It must have been hard on Harold to be separated from Ena. She was in many ways his support system. He must have been plagued with guilt, for he had involved her in a horrible mess, while she had loyally given him as much assistance as she could. Or such was the case if his story rings true.

Almost as soon as Harold Nokes was jailed, he was examined by a doctor. His blood pressure had rocketed upward to extremely dangerous levels, and medication did not relieve the condition. Nokes, alone in the jail, moped in his cell. He tried to engage Roblee in conversation, but Roblee was non-committal. There was nothing for Harold to do but think. The *Gazette* reported on December 26 that Roblee had advised them that Nokes was "depressed." Harold Nokes was alone with Roblee and the deputies who were there from time to time. Harold barely touched his food, and according to Roblee, "He looked awful." Nokes finally pried one of the lenses out of his glasses and attempted to cut his wrist. Roblee heard him trying to sharpen the lens by rubbing it against the rough floor of his cell and confiscated the lens and glasses, but not until after Harold had succeeded in drawing blood from his wrist.

Roblee suspected that sooner or later Nokes would want to clear his conscience. Roblee fashioned a large placard out of cardboard that contained the Miranda warnings—stating that anything that Harold said could be used against him, that he need say nothing at all, and that he was entitled to counsel—and hung it in the jail so that it was always visible from Nokes's cell. Whenever Harold tried to engage Roblee in conversation about any aspect of the crime, Roblee would point to the sign and warn Nokes of his rights.

Finally, on December 27, a week after he had been jailed, a week of listening to the generator and scarcely eating, Harold Nokes indicated to Roblee that he wanted to talk about the Hoyts. Nokes had received a visit that day from his lawyer, Richard Hove, who was en route to Colorado for a skiing vacation. Hove had visited Ena earlier the same day and had apparently related some information about her to Harold.

From listening to the Nokeses' conversation during the bugging process, Roblee knew that the suicide trigger was for Ena to get word to Harold that her back hurt. They would both then take the codeine pills. Harold no longer had his stash of pills but was unaware that Ena did not.

After Hove had departed, Roblee asked Harold if the lawyer had brought any news of Ena. Roblee then said that Hove had told him he had forgotten to tell Harold that Ena had been complaining about back pain. The ploy worked to perfection.

It may well be that Harold thought Ena had gone forward with the plan to commit suicide, and he was unable to carry out his end of the pact. After considering this news for some time, Harold proceeded to tell Roblee, in great detail, the facts of the murders and the dismemberment.

Nokes talked, and Roblee listened. He interjected an occasional question but did not take notes, having no desire to shut off the flow of information. Roblee said it was apparent that as he talked, Harold felt a great sense of relief, as though a great weight was being lifted from his shoulders. So visible was the change, that Roblee arranged for another blood pressure check. The next day, a doctor's visit established that Nokes's blood pressure had returned to normal. His appetite immediately improved.

After Harold had finished cleansing his conscience, Roblee contacted Fred Schroeder and informed him of the confession. Because it was now known that the murders had taken place in McCook, the charges against the Nokeses would have to be refiled in Red Willow County. Schroeder also called Richard Hove and Paul Douglas, and the parties began to engage in plea bargaining, both for Harold and for Ena, a process that lasted several days. Red Willow County attorney Clyde Starrett, remembering the Ida Fitzgibbons case, was only too happy to let Schroeder and Douglas do the lion's share of the work.

Relying on Harold Nokes's oral confession to Roblee, all parties agreed that two counts of murder would be filed against Harold: second-degree murder in the case of Edwin Hoyt, because Harold had not had sufficient time to form an intent to murder Hoyt, and first-degree murder in the case of Wilma Hoyt, because he had had time to form an intent. Harold was adamant that Ena was not involved, and the plea bargaining resulted in two counts of wrongful disposal of a dead body being filed against her, one for each of the Hoyts.

The prosecution agreed not to make any recommendation as to whether the sentences should run consecutively or concurrently and to make no recommendation as to the penalty . . . life or death . . . on the first-degree murder count. Through his lawyer, Nokes agreed to the deal and agreed to make a statement outlining the facts of the crimes.

At Schroeder's office in Curtis on January 4, 1974, six days after his initial confession to Roblee, Harold Nokes gave a 158-page statement in the presence of Douglas, Roblee, and Hove. Douglas brought a court reporter from Lincoln to transcribe the confession. The statement opened with a discussion of the plea bargain, and Douglas agreed that no matter what Harold Nokes said in the statement, no greater charges than wrongful disposal of dead bodies would be filed against Ena. It was clear to all those present that Harold Nokes would not participate unless Ena was protected. It has never been clarified if Harold confessed to Roblee because he believed that Ena had committed suicide or how and when he learned that she had not. If he thought she had died when he confessed to Roblee, he never admitted it in any of his statements. If Harold thought Ena was dead, why did he not attempt to blame the killings on her?

Ena has never spoken of her role in the murders. No doubt Roblee notified Hove that Harold had confessed, and no doubt Hove so informed Ena. But neither can recall. If Ena did not learn immediately that Harold had done his best to plea bargain in her behalf, she must have had anxious moments until she learned of the lesser charges filed against her.

The story that Harold Nokes told to Douglas and Roblee in his statement for the court reporter was, from all appearances, a laconic and straightforward account of what transpired during the killing and dismemberment of the Hoyts. The matter-of-fact, prosaic language is chilling, as is shown in the following colloquies. There is nothing in his words to indicate that Harold was under any stress. Such was Douglas's recollection as well. Yet Nokes must have been anxious as he told his story to an experienced and aggressive prosecutor.

Harold explained that on Sunday, September 23, the day of the murders, he and Ena had dinner at the home of his brother in McCook. Harold's parents were there, as were his brother and sister-in-law. Harold could not remember if his sister and her husband were also there, but he thought they were. After eating, Harold and Ena returned home and did not go out again until around 7:30 or 8:00 p.m., when they went to a drive-in restaurant for a sandwich.

Next, according to Harold, they drove to Culbertson to see his parents. When they arrived in Culbertson, likely around 9:00 p.m., Harold's parents' home was dark, so he and Ena decided instead to go to the home of Mr. and Mrs. Hoyt.

What if the lights had been on? Would they have stopped to see the elder Nokeses and perhaps visited for a while? Harold indicated that they had made the trip to Culbertson because his father had been ill. Had his condition deteriorated since noon? Harold knew when they left their house that evening, though, that he and Ena were going to see the Hoyts. In his statement Harold explained that he took his pistol to the Hoyt farm for protection. "My shoulder was such that I knew that he [Edwin Hoyt] might get violent, and I took a gun along, just figured that if there was trouble I might stop trouble and get away from there without any trouble."

Harold explained that he was carrying his loaded pistol tucked into his belt under his jacket. Douglas pressed him further on this point:

Q. Okay. Now, where were you when you made up your mind you were going to go over and see Mr. Hoyt to get the misunderstanding straightened out?

A. That was before we left home, I guess. I decided from there to go by the folks and see if they was all right, and if they wasn't I would probably go out and see if they were home.

Q. And suppose your folks were all right, would you have stayed there and talked with your folks?

A. If they would have been up, I would have probably stopped and I would have probably stopped and I probably wouldn't have gone out there.

Q. And you wouldn't have gone to the Hoyts?

A. Probably not that night, no.

Because Harold Nokes confessed, no effort was made to check with the drive-in restaurant to see if anyone remembered Harold and Ena Nokes coming for a sandwich on Sunday evening. The trip to the home of the elder Nokeses, whom they had seen at noon, may well have been a fabrication to make it seem as if the Nokeses arrived at the Hoyt farm later than they had. The Hoyts had received the phone call from their son in the navy at Charleston, South Carolina, at about 7:30 that evening. After this brief call the activities of the Hoyts for the rest of the evening, until they were murdered at the Nokeses' house, are unknown. In response to a question from Douglas, Harold outlined the sequence of events after leaving the Hoyts' home:

Q. Okay. So now, the purpose in going to your house
was what, at that point?

A. We went to my house and thought we would call
Kay over, and then we could clarify what was right and
what was wrong.

Why not go directly to Kay's house? What was she going
to do with her girls if she received a telephone call at 10:00
on a Sunday night?

Q. Okay, so as you walked into the house, where did
you go?

A. From the time we entered the house, why, then, Mr.
Hoyt was getting pretty loud with his conversation, and
I made some remark to the fact that we didn't want
all the neighbors to know we were having trouble or
something; if we were going to make so much noise
we should go to the basement or something. And he
just took off for the basement. And, so . . .

Q. He knew how to get down the stairs?

A. He must have because he went that way anyway.

Harold said that Edwin Hoyt appeared ready to hit him
and was coming toward him at the time he shot Hoyt. "I
would say from the time he laid his glasses down, he would
probably be eight feet or so from where I was at, eight, ten
feet. Probably eight feet."

Q. When you pulled the gun out, how did you hold it?

A. Well, I just pulled it out with my left-hand and
pointed it at him. I thought it . . .

Q. How close to you did he get?

A. He was just ready to hit me when I fired.

Q. Three feet, four feet?

A. I would say three feet.

An average sized man could cover the five foot distance between eight feet and three feet in a stride and a half. For the right-handed Harold Nokes to pull the pistol from his belt with his left hand, aim it, release the safety, and fire, that would have been a performance worthy of Wild Bill Hickok. Sheriff Roblee, who was present at the confession, thought so as well. He asked Harold about the safety. Nokes replied, "If it is on safe, there is a little clip. I had it loaded, and all I had to do was clip the safe off and it was ready to go." Roblee pressed him:

Q. Which side is the safe on, on that thing?
A. I never used it enough that I . . . to be right sure, but I think it would be on the left side of the pistol, but I am not . . .
Q. How would you run it with your left hand?
A. I don't know whether I reached, did it off with my right hand or not, I just don't know. It happened so quick that I couldn't tell you, I honestly don't know . . .

Douglas asked Nokes about the death of Wilma Hoyt:

Q. Did she go to her husband?
A. No, she started screaming and started up the stairs.
Q. And all she said to you was "Why didn't you kill Kay?"
A. Yes, that's right.
Q. And started going up the stairs?
A. Yes.
Q. And then what happened?
A. Then I shot her.

Douglas questioned Nokes about the dismemberment of the bodies:

Q. For instance, I could understand how you did the limbs, but after you got rid of the four limbs, what would you do with the main body itself?

A. Well, I had to break the bone up through here, and then ...

Q. Up through here, you are talking about the chest bone?

A. Yes

Q. Through the middle of the chest?

A. Yes, and then I had to cut down the back so that the front and the back were separated, so I had two halves. And then, I cut those probably in three pieces across through here so each side was probably, I would guess, in three pieces, I don't know.

Douglas then took Nokes through the disposal of the bodies in the lake, especially concerning the heads:

Q. Now, as you were dumping them, how about the heads which is the part that I am really interested in, do you recall what you know as you unwrapped them, you certainly would have noticed which part the heads were.

A. Certainly

Q. What did you do with the heads?

A. Put them in with the rest of it.

Q. Right down in the middle of the lake.

A. Yes.

During his oral confession to Roblee, Harold said he had taken the heads of Edwin and Wilma Hoyt to an area where a creek entered Strunk Lake and trampled them deep into the mud. Harold was not asked to explain this discrepancy while the reported confession was being taken, even though Roblee was present. The heads, three feet, and the spines of the two bodies have never surfaced. Trampling the heads in the mud of the creek would have soaked and soiled Harold Nokes's trousers, which would have raised questions if anyone had been at the lake during the evening of disposal and had seen him dripping and muddy. In any event, he changed his story between his oral confession to Roblee and the written confession. When the written confession was almost finished, Douglas asked Roblee if what Nokes had said was the same as what he had told Roblee. Roblee's response was, "That sounds just like what he told me."

Of course, Roblee did not take notes while Nokes was pouring out his story. However, it does seem unusual that something as important as the disposal of the heads would not have jogged Roblee's memory.

After Harold had finished his confession to Douglas and the court reporter, Douglas asked Nokes if he would be willing to take a lie detector test if his attorney had no objection. Nokes immediately went on the defensive and said it would not be necessary, as everything that he had told Douglas was the truth.

Douglas told Nokes, "I find it very difficult to believe a lot of things that you told me." Douglas questioned why Harold took his gun to the Hoyts' and why the parties went to the basement upon arriving at the Nokeses' home. Douglas was also troubled by the fact that Wilma Hoyt was supposed to call Kay to have her come to the Nokeses' house, though there was no phone in the Nokeses' basement. Douglas did not raise the even more basic question, why didn't they call Kay from the Hoyt farm before driving to McCook?

Earlier in the confession, Douglas asked Harold if he and Ena had discussed the events of the murders and agreed on a version of the story to use with the authorities. Harold replied that the killings had dominated their conversations and that he was sure Ena would tell them the same story he had, although he did not know if she was aware he had taken his gun to the Hoyts'.

If that discussion had been carried to its logical conclusion, Douglas would have talked to Ena before Schroeder filed the charges in McCook against the guilty pair. Perhaps Hove would have objected to such a conversation, as Ena might have revealed enough to have justified first-degree murder charges against Harold on both killings, rather than just on Wilma Hoyt. If Ena had known Harold had taken a gun to the Hoyt house or if she knew he planned to use it, Harold would have been in very hot water as to the intent to kill. And Ena could scarcely refuse to talk, since a plea bargain had already been struck on her behalf. Douglas had even said as much at the outset of the confession as an inducement for Harold to tell his story. Why Douglas allowed Ena to remain silent is perplexing.

On January 10, 1974, Schroeder filed documents charging Harold Nokes with one count of first-degree murder and one count of second-degree murder and Ena Nokes with two counts of the wrongful disposal of a dead body. The written informations, the technical legal term for the charges, against Harold and Ena alleged the facts of the killing and the disposal of the bodies. Harold Nokes entered pleas of guilty to each count the same day, a preliminary hearing having been waived, and Judge Hendrix found him guilty on both counts. Ena Nokes pleaded nolo contendere, or no contest, to both counts and was found guilty on both counts. Thus no trial of either was necessary, and only sentencing remained.

While waiting for their sentencing, the Nokeses took steps to secure their property. They transferred the title of their car to their son, Al, and on January 3, 1974, they transferred their home at 903 Avenue G to their son and daughter in trust. (On April 11, 1974, the Nokeses' children sold the home for $12,000 to two local residents.) Ena was released on bond on January 17, after having posted $25,000 in U.S. government bonds as security. The relatively low amount of bail reflected the success of Harold's plea bargaining on her behalf. After she was released on bond, she was able to oversee the closing of the house and prepared the Nokeses' marital assets for safeguarding.

Judge Hendrix set February 14 as the date for Ena's sentencing. At the sentencing hearing, Harold Bennett, the McCook superintendent of schools, and Ruth Leopold, the school's business manager and Ena's immediate supervisor, both testified as character witnesses on Ena's behalf, stressing her dependability, efficiency, and absence of any criminal record. No one appeared against her. Following the hearing, Judge Hendrix sentenced Ena to three years on the first count and two years on the second, the sentences to be served consecutively at the women's prison in York, Nebraska.

In a judicial order filed January 16, Judge Hendrix determined that since the death penalty on the first-degree charge was an option in Harold's case, a three-judge panel would be convened on February 28 to pass sentence. On January 21 Chief Justice Paul White of the Nebraska Supreme Court appointed district judges Herbert Ronin of Lincoln and William Colwell of Pawnee City to the sentencing panel, along with Hendrix.

William Colwell was a former FBI agent. After leaving the bureau, he practiced law in Pawnee City, located in extreme southeastern Nebraska, and then became a district judge. Lawyers in his area and fellow judges acknowledged his intelligence and good judgment. As a former FBI agent, he was knowledgeable about firearms. Because of his judicial ability and his light case load, he was often called to sit with the Nebraska Supreme Court when one of the judges was unable to participate.

Herbert Ronin, the third member of the sentencing panel, was probably the most well-known Mason in Nebraska. A county judge before moving up to the district bench, he was gracious, thoughtful, and optimistic. Tall and balding, he moved with a shambling gait and was always willing to stop and visit.

None of the three men had ever individually imposed a death sentence. Nebraska law at the time required that if the death penalty was an option in a case, three judges, rather than just the trial judge, had to determine whether the aggravating factors spelled out in the death penalty law outweighed mitigating factors in the case, before they could impose the death penalty.

Such procedures were necessitated when, in 1972 in a Georgia case titled *Furman v. Georgia*, the U.S. Supreme Court ruled that death sentences across the United States were being disproportionately imposed and suspended the imposition of the death penalty nationwide. The court clearly felt that the death penalty was imposed far more often for minority defendants than white defendants and for crimes that were intensified by the social and economic status of the victim.

As a result of the Supreme Court decision, the Nebraska legislature followed the lead of Georgia and adopted new death penalty statutes that spelled out nine aggravating circumstances and seven mitigating circumstances that had to be weighed against each other in order to determine if the imposition of the death penalty was justified.

The procedures for imposing a death sentence in Nebraska

have now changed. The Nebraska Supreme Court has held that the electric chair, the only method of execution authorized by Nebraska law, constitutes cruel and unusual punishment under the Nebraska constitution. Responding to the court's decision, the Nebraska legislature has adopted lethal injection as the sole authorized form of execution in Nebraska. The Nebraska Supreme Court has not yet ruled on the constitutionality of lethal injection.

Because of subsequent decisions of the U.S. Supreme Court, it is now necessary for the jury that finds a defendant guilty of first-degree murder to determine, in a separate hearing, whether any aggravating circumstances exist. Their finding is then given to the three-judge sentencing panel, which holds a hearing to determine if any mitigating factors exist, before weighing the factors. If the jury does not find any aggravating factors, the sentencing panel cannot impose the death penalty.

At the time of the Hoyt murders, the aggravating circumstances were as follows:

a. The offender was previously convicted of another murder or a crime involving the use or threat of violence to the person, or has a substantial prior history of serious assaultive or terrorizing criminal activity.

b. The murder was committed in an effort to conceal the commission of a crime, or to conceal the identity of the perpetrator of such crime.

c. The murder was committed for hire, or for pecuniary gain, or the defendant hired another to commit the murder for the defendant.

d. The murder was especially heinous, atrocious, cruel, or manifested exceptional depravity by ordinary standards of morality and intelligence.

e. At the time the murder was committed, the offender also committed another murder.

f. The offender knowingly created a great risk of death to at least several persons.

g. The victim was a public servant having lawful custody of the offender or another in the lawful performance of his or her official duties and the offender knew or should have known that the victim was a public servant performing his or her official duties.

h. The murder was committed knowingly to disrupt or hinder the lawful exercise of any governmental function or the enforcement of the laws.

The mitigating circumstances were as follows:

a. The offender has no significant history or prior criminal activity.

b. The offender acted under unusual pressures or influences or under the domination of another person.

c. The crime was committed while the offender was under the influence of extreme mental or emotional disturbance.

d. The age of the defendant at the time of the crime.

e. The offender was an accomplice in the crime committed by another person and his or her participation was relatively minor.

f. The victim was a participant in the defendant's conduct or consented to the act.

g. At the time of the crime, the capacity of the defendant to appreciate the wrongfulness of his or her conduct or to conform his or her conduct to the requirements of law was impaired as a result of mental illness, mental defect, or intoxication.

On February 28 a sentencing hearing was held for Harold at the county courthouse in McCook. Lincoln and Omaha media were present in force, and 150 McCook citizens crowded into the room. The court received a voluminous presentencing report prepared by Arthur Cook, the chief probation officer of the Ninth Judicial District. The report contained 180 letters to the court regarding the sentencing of the Nokeses. Among the missives, many written by relatives of Harold and Ena, were letters from retired district judge Victor Westermark, and retired county judge Wendell Cheney. Westermark made no sentencing recommendation but said Harold was from a good family, while Cheney complimented Ena's character and her work in the assessor's office. Only one of the letters, signed from "a taxpayer and citizen of McCook," contained any detrimental material, urging that the Nokeses receive the maximum penalty. Virtually all the other letters were glowing in their praise of Harold and Ena. The collection of letters appeared to be the result of a carefully orchestrated campaign by the Nokeses' children to inundate the probation officer with material beneficial to the Nokeses. Over forty relatives—including the Nokeses' son and daughter, Ena's mother, and a conglomeration of aunts, brothers, and cousins—all wrote with their support, as did many residents of Danbury and both Harold's and Ena's coworkers. Judge William Colwell, the only member of the sentencing panel still living, discounted the report and said it was of very little help to the panel because of its obvious bias.

Only one witness testified at the sentencing hearing. Dr. Louis Martin, a psychiatrist at the Hastings Regional Center, had been hired by Hove to examine and evaluate Harold two days before the hearing. Martin was not familiar with the complete contents of Harold's confession and had only seen him briefly, yet he stated that Harold Nokes was "under unusual pressure" at the time of the slayings because of his feelings for Kay. Martin did not specify the nature of the pressure more fully, nor did he testify that Harold was mentally ill.

Harold Nokes also testified at the hearing. Rather than speaking of the Hoyt murders, Harold said only that he did not paint all the graffiti slandering Kay—an astonishing irrelevancy. Paul Douglas objected to some of the questions Hove asked Dr. Martin but did not make any objections to Harold's testimony and offered no argument as to sentence, as he had agreed in the plea bargain. Why Hove made no effort to ask for mercy for his client is puzzling. Hove had told the *Lincoln Journal* even before the hearing that he was not going to call Harold Nokes to the stand. But Harold Nokes was disturbed that Douglas had implied Nokes painted all the obscene messages, and he wanted to respond. Virtually all defense lawyers put their perpetrator on the stand to apologize and to attempt to show they were in the grip of strong passion. Nothing in the plea bargain would have prevented Harold Nokes from making similar statements. Harold stated in his confession that he did not paint all the messages about Kay and that he had seen several before he painted any himself. Why he was so concerned about his reputation regarding the graffiti, when he was a confessed murderer and butcher, is hard to comprehend. Perhaps he did not want to further offend those sexual partners of Kay who had been mentioned in the painted graffiti. The *Lincoln Journal* reported that after the hearing was over, Harold had a brief meeting with Ena. As the *Journal* described, "Nokes advised his wife to stop putting it off and get started with serving her prison sentence."

Ena did as Harold requested, surrendering to the court after the completion of the sentencing hearing. The $25,000 in bonds that she had posted was returned to her, since she had appeared for sentencing. Ena was sent to the York prison for women immediately thereafter and began serving her sentence. Hove appealed the sentences on Ena's behalf, on the grounds that the sentences should have run concurrently rather than consecutively, but the Nebraska Supreme Court dismissed the appeal on July 17, 1974, for failure to file briefs, the written assignments of error and the arguments that allow the supreme court to review the lower court proceedings. She was paroled on June 8, 1976, and discharged from parole on August 22, 1977. No record exists of testimony at either the parole or discharge hearing, but it can be assumed that she comported herself lawfully. She moved to Lincoln and has resided there since her release.

The court set March 22, 1974, as the date for Harold's sentence to be imposed; on that Thursday morning, before a packed courtroom of some two hundred locals and representatives of the media, the three judges met to hand down their sentencing decision. Reporters from as far away as Kansas City, Missouri, were present. The press coverage of the sensational case had continued unabated since September. The *McCook Gazette* had a field day with the story, and the metropolitan dailies from Omaha and Lincoln stayed on top of the case as well.

National print media covered the events as well. On November 14 the *Gazette* advised its readers that *Newsweek* was in town for a story on the murders, and on November 21 the *Gazette* reported on the heavy demand for copies of *Newsweek* in the McCook area. The *Newsweek* story focused on cult activity in McCook, and on November 26 the *Gazette* reported the Hoyts' pastor at the Culbertson Methodist Church stated that *Newsweek* had incorrectly quoted him as to the disposition of the severed heads of the Hoyts.

The most comprehensive newspaper account appeared in the *Kansas City Times* on January 17, 1974, written by staff writer Kathleen Patterson. The story appeared after Harold Nokes's confession and before both the sentencing hearing on February 28 and the imposition of sentence on March 22. The article captures the mood of McCook and the surprise of the Nokeses' neighbors and provides an accurate summary of what transpired on the fateful night of September 23. Photos in the *Times* of the major players (Douglas, Schroeder, and the Nokeses) and of a snow-covered Strunk Lake caught the venue and the attitude of southwestern Nebraska frozen in a brief moment in time. Subtly, it differentiated the Hoyt murders from the Clutter murders in western Kansas that had so challenged Truman Capote in his masterful *In Cold Blood*.

The three judges had jurisdiction over only the first-degree murder count in the death of Wilma Hoyt. Because the second-degree charge for the death of Edwin Hoyt did not involve the death penalty, Judge Hendrix would impose that sentence himself. Harold Nokes, who had been sequestered at the penitentiary in Lincoln since his arraignment, returned to McCook for the hearing and anxiously awaited the sentence. It was not long in coming.

Prior to deciding on Nokes's sentence, the three judges met in chambers to discuss among themselves the presence of the statutory aggravating and mitigating circumstances. They determined that two aggravating circumstances applied to the murder of Wilma Hoyt: (b) the murder was committed to conceal the commission of a crime and (e) another murder was committed at the same time. As to circumstance (d), which has fostered more litigation than any of the other aggravators, the panel found, "We are manifestly cognizant of the horrible inhumane mutilation and disposition of the body, but the legislature has restricted consideration of this by prefacing the requirements with, 'The murder was,' and requiring the court to consider, for this circumstance, only the murder itself. That the cutting of the body was done after death is confirmed by medical evidence in the record and could not have been a part of the murder."

The panel also found two mitigating circumstances: (a) Nokes's prior pristine criminal record and (c) the crime was committed while Nokes was under the influence of extreme mental or emotional disturbance. The court said in its finding as to (e), "This defendant, with his particular personality, the sexual and emotional involvement he had entered into with the daughter of the victim, and his immature reaction to his rejection as a lover made it obvious that his mental and emotional disturbance was of the greatest extremity."

The panel found that the two mitigating circumstances approached or exceeded the weight to be given to the two aggravating circumstances. The three-judge panel concluded that the murder itself was not especially heinous. The heinous dismemberment of the bodies occurred after death had taken place, and as the judges saw it, that did not fit within the statutory definition of aggravation. Accordingly, the panel sentenced Harold Nokes to life imprisonment rather than choosing the death penalty. Judge Hendrix, who also imposed a life sentence on the count of second-degree murder, decreed that the sentences should run consecutively.

After his sentencing Harold Nokes returned to the state penitentiary, where he remains today. In his interview with the author, the only interview he has granted in the thirty-nine years of his imprisonment, Nokes stated that Schroeder and an officer of the state parole board both advised him that he would be out of prison after serving no more than twenty years. The men believed that the State of Nebraska Board of Pardons, consisting of the governor, the attorney general, and the secretary of state would commute Harold's sentences to a term of years, so he would then be eligible for parole. The pardons board commuted thirty-two life sentences between 1973 and 1990. But the pardons board threw Harold Nokes a curve when, in 1990, it adopted a policy to no longer commute life sentences to a term of years. In Nebraska, at present, a life sentence means just that—life in prison.

Judge Colwell, in an interview with the author, stated that it was apparent to him from the outset that Judge Hendrix did not believe that Harold Nokes should receive the death penalty and that Hendrix believed he was mirroring the prevailing mood of McCook. In a telephone interview, Hendrix's daughter said her father opposed the death penalty, because it was final and if mistakes had occurred in the legal process, they could not be rectified. Once the hysteria over the murders had died down and the culprits had been identified, Hendrix felt the townspeople of McCook remembered that they had always liked Harold and Ena Nokes. In addition, all three of the judges were aware that the Nebraska Supreme Court had not issued an opinion on the new aggravating-mitigating standards. Thus the panel was wading into uncharted waters.

Colwell felt that Harold Nokes's sexual activity played no part in the sentence, and he thought whether Nokes had taken the pistol with him when he went to see the Hoyts was the great unanswered question in the case. But the other judges were willing to follow Hendrix's lead.

On April 15, 1974, two months after the sentencing, James Kelley, a Lincoln attorney, filed on behalf of Harold Nokes in district court a notice of appeal of the sentences. Richard Hove was no longer Nokes's attorney. Whether he withdrew of his own accord or was dismissed by Harold is not clear. Hove says his work was done, and there was no need to appeal or any rational basis for doing so. In an interview with the author, Kelley stated that the Nokeses' daughter, Sharon Ignowski, hired him to prosecute an appeal because of discrepancies appearing in Hove's bill. Harold Nokes repeated the same allegation in his interview.

Harold Nokes's contention was that Hove had charged a substantial amount for conferring with another lawyer. Sharon Ignowski, however, knew the other lawyer and learned that the conference consisted of only one phone call. Hove denies the allegations and insists he charged Harold Nokes a fixed fee at the outset, which Nokes paid, and never billed the Nokeses again for any amount.

In his argument before the Nebraska Supreme Court in the fall of 1974, Kelley raised three issues. He argued that there was no factual basis for charging first-degree murder in the death of Wilma Hoyt, because it had happened so rapidly that it was an instinctive response, with no time for Harold Nokes to formulate intent. He also contended that Hove had given Harold ineffective assistance in failing to file motions to suppress evidence garnered from the wire taps, which he stated were not justified. Finally, he maintained that it was an abuse of discretion to impose sentences to run consecutively.

The supreme court made short work of Kelley's argument, releasing their opinion on February 2, 1975. Judge Hale McCown, a highly regarded member of the court, wrote the opinion, stating that a guilty plea, if voluntarily made, as Harold Nokes's was, waives all defenses to the charge whether they be procedural, statutory, or constitutional. Judge McCown also found that there was no valid reason why a public policy of retribution, leading to a maximum sentence, was not warranted in Harold Nokes's case.

On April 29, 1980, counsel for Harold Nokes filed a motion for postconviction relief, a procedural step made when challenging the results of the prosecution of a case. In district court in McCook, Harold Nokes was represented by a third lawyer, Duane Nelson of Lincoln. Neither Hove nor Kelley was a participant. Why Nokes selected a new lawyer is not known, although Nelson had been involved in the Ida Fitzgibbons case. Judge Hendrix, after reviewing the case file and testimonial record, overruled the motion without granting an evidentiary hearing. Nelson appealed to the Nebraska Supreme Court.

On appeal Nelson alleged that there had been ineffective assistance by Hove and that the guilty plea was not voluntary. The supreme court reviewed Judge McCown's opinion on the direct appeal and found that both issues had been raised then and had been decided against Nokes. The supreme court affirmed the decision of the district court, stating that the postconviction act was intended only to hear issues that had not been raised in the direct appeal and that it did not allow a further review of issues already litigated. The opinion was released on June 26, 1981. If Hove had been ineffective in his defense or if the guilty plea had been coerced, a habeas corpus action in federal court might have given Harold Nokes an avenue for a hearing, but no doubt Nelson, a former assistant U.S. attorney, did not think the chances of success in that venue justified filing such an action.

The judicial epic thus came to an end. Harold Nokes remains at the penitentiary, where he operates a computer in the prison photo lab. He appears reconciled to ending his days behind bars. But a multitude of questions exist. Did the killings happen as Harold has related, or is there a darker side to the story? Were each of the Hoyts killed with only one shot? Could a right-handed man with only minimal use of his right arm swing an ax with his left hand with sufficient force to dismember bodies and sever heads? Could he pull a pistol from his belt with his left hand, release the safety, and fire before an onrushing victim could cover a distance of three feet? Why does Harold Nokes deny today that he and Ena carried on a sexual affair with Kay Hein but admits that he had sex with Kay at his home while Ena was present and with her knowledge?

7

The Problems

What is known about the Hoyt murders pales in comparison with what is not. It is very likely that Harold Nokes did not tell the true story of what happened to end the lives of Edwin and Wilma Hoyt. What is even more likely is that the reasons for their death and mutilation will never be discovered. But a respect for the truth, for the tragic circumstances that brought all the actors together at the same time and place, leads one to carefully scrutinize the people and the possibilities.

To begin, there are vast discrepancies between the story Harold Nokes related to his captors before he was sentenced and the story he told in September of 2007, some thirty-three odd years later. Nokes was interviewed at the Nebraska State Penitentiary by the author, the only interview he has given since his confinement early in 1974. The interview was conducted in the presence of Win Barber, administrative assistant to the warden of the penitentiary, and was tape-recorded.

Harold Nokes has certainly had ample time to reflect on the events of the fateful night. But he is an old man now, and memory fades with the passage of time. Details that were once etched on his consciousness have faded. Perhaps in an effort to put together a version of the tragedy that he can live with, in an effort to cast himself in his own mind in the most favorable light possible, he has concocted a sanitized version of what really took place. But a comparison of what he said then and what he says now is disturbing.

Nokes told his prosecutors that he took his .22-caliber pistol to the Hoyt home on the night of September 23, 1973. He stated that the gun was fully loaded with a nine-shot clip, that there was a round in the chamber, that the gun was cocked, and that the safety was on. Those who knew Harold Nokes described him as a true sportsman, an avid hunter, who participated in several hunting groups. Tucking a loaded handgun in the waistband of one's trousers with a bullet in firing position, cocked and ready to fire but for the safety, is an action that goes against virtually every facet of firearms safety. An accidental firing could injure himself or someone in the vicinity.

Harold Nokes had from September, when the murders occurred, until late December, when he confessed, to put together a story that would cast him in the most favorable light. It is entirely possible—indeed, probable—that the killings did not take place as he outlined in his statement. Instead, Harold may have taken the Hoyts to his basement at gunpoint, selecting the concrete-floored laundry room as an easily cleaned place of execution. Both of the Hoyts might have been killed there.

Harold Nokes's account of how he drew the gun, released the safety, and fired, as Edwin Hoyt was moving toward him in the basement, needs to be analyzed and questioned, but it was his story when he confessed.

The gun used in the killings was the .22-caliber Ruger pistol Harold Nokes had purchased in August. It had a nine-shot magazine that fit into the hollow handle. The pistol has a long, narrow barrel and resembles the Luger pistol carried by Nazi officers in World War II. Ruger is a well-known and popular firearms manufacturer, and the Germanic-appearing pistol was a best seller for many years, although the configuration has now changed drastically, with a much shorter barrel.

The gun was loaded and cocked when Harold tucked it in his belt earlier that evening. The safety on the pistol is at the left rear, where it is easily thumbed off by a shooter holding it in his right hand. But Harold said that as Edwin approached him with a cocked fist, he pulled the gun with his left hand—Nokes is right-handed—released the safety, and pulled the trigger before Hoyt could cover three feet, one stride.

In a test conducted with the assistance of the Lincoln, Nebraska, police department, in an effort to test the credibility of Harold Nokes's claim, it proved impossible to pull the pistol, release the safety, and fire in such a short interval of time. There is a sight on the muzzle end of the barrel, and the sight caught on the shooter's belt on several instances. With the left index finger through the trigger guard, it was not possible to reach over the top of the barrel with the left hand and release the safety, no matter the length of time involved. The physical difficulty involved in drawing and firing as Harold Nokes stated makes it a virtual certainty that the shooting of Edwin Hoyt did not take place as he related.

During Harold Nokes's confession to Douglas—which took place at the Frontier County law office of county attorney Fred Schroeder and in the presence of Douglas, Sheriff Lannie Roblee, the court reporter, and Dick Hove—Lannie Roblee asked Nokes if the gun was cocked while it was tucked in his belt. He replied that it was not. However, Harold stated that he had drawn the gun with his left hand, released the safety, and fired, meaning the gun would already have been cocked. Roblee queried Nokes extensively about whether the safety was on and how he had released the safety. Harold was evasive in his reply, speculating that he might have reached over the barrel with his right hand.

Nokes subsequently stated that he had practiced with the

pistol a few times using his left hand, but he must have been skilled indeed to have killed the Hoyts with only one shot each. It is quite possible that the entire clip was fired during the murders. Not enough of the Hoyts' bodies remained to give testimony to the number of shots used to kill them.

When questioned at the penitentiary, Nokes denied taking the gun to the Hoyt home. Instead, Harold said that when he and the Hoyts reached the Nokeses' house, Edwin went immediately to the basement. Harold then went to his bedroom and removed the pistol out of a dresser drawer before following Edwin to the basement. Such a story raises several questions. Had Edwin Hoyt ever been in the basement before? Why would he agree to go to the basement? Why did Harold think he needed a gun? Was the gun loaded and cocked while lying in the dresser drawer?

It seems more credible to argue, as Harold stated in his confession, that he was the one who suggested going to the basement. Did he have the gun secreted on his person when they arrived at the house, or did he take it from his dresser in order to diminish the anger of the irate Hoyt?

In his confession, Nokes detailed the steps he took in dissecting the bodies, packaging the parts, and disposing of the body parts in Strunk Lake. In his interview at the penitentiary, he stated he blacked out after the shootings and could not remember cutting up the bodies but could remember throwing the parts in the lake. He denied, in the interview, what he had said in his confession about going back to the lake to see if any parts had surfaced. He was quite clear, however, in the interview that Ena was not involved in any way with the dismemberment of the bodies.

Though Harold Nokes is shrunken now, he was a good-sized man in 1973—six feet two inches and 210 pounds. He was involved in physical outdoor work on a daily basis, and photos of him at the time indicate he was in good shape. But during his confession he maintained that he had essentially lost the use of his right arm and hand. He stated that he beheaded the bodies by gripping an ax halfway up the handle and swinging it with his left hand. Swinging an ax with enough force to cut a head from a torso when a body is lying on a concrete floor runs a substantial risk of a dangerous ricochet as the ax blade bounces off the concrete.

For a right-handed person, even one experienced at butchering and dressing game, cutting through the bone and gristle of a torso with a butcher knife in one's left hand presents formidable obstacles. Sawdon and the state patrol had earlier elicited from Ena Nokes that she had field dressed and butchered a deer, and she had described the process step-by-step. If Harold Nokes was as disabled as he said he was in his confession, and as he now maintains, it defies belief that Ena Nokes's participation in the slaughter was confined to merely wrapping the body parts in freezer paper. But both then and now, Nokes has maintained that such was the case.

No traces of blood were ever found in the police's extensive search of the house. But neither was any blood found at the Hoyt home, in the Hoyt car, or in either of the Nokeses' vehicles. If the killings and dissection did take place in the washroom, as Harold related, Ena proved to be a gimlet-eyed cleaning lady, removing every incriminating trace of flesh and blood.

Of course, forensic science has improved exponentially since 1973, and it is likely that if the killings had taken place today, the floor and drain of the Nokeses' home would have yielded their grisly secrets. The Nokeses' house was not searched by authorities until early October, meaning Ena would have had some two weeks to remove every vestige of the butchery.

Harold Nokes's court-reported confession is replete with references to the plea bargain that he and his lawyer had made with the prosecutors. The agreement stated that no matter what action might be taken against Harold, Ena would only be charged with the wrongful disposal of two dead bodies, not acting as an abettor or accomplice in two counts of murder. Why was he so interested in protecting Ena? Was it the act of a loving husband or of a man who had carried on an illicit affair for two years before telling his wife? The authorities were well aware of the sexual triangle. Both Harold and Kay Hein had provided the details of the arrangement two months before Harold confessed. He could not hope to paint Ena as a passive participant given the detail he and Kay had already furnished. Was he worried that Ena might reveal that he had shot the Hoyts multiple times, thus clearly demonstrating a calculated intent to murder?

Most startling of all the changes in Nokes's story between the confession and the recent interview was Nokes's account of his sexual activity with Kay Hein. In the interview, he unequivocally denied the existence of the sexual threesome. He insisted that Ena was never involved in any sexual relationship with him and Kay, a relationship that both he and Kay had told to the authorities in graphic detail before the confession and that he reiterated in the confession.

Harold Nokes acknowledged to the author that he had had an affair with Kay but claimed it was infrequent and did not take place in motels, only in his car or home. He stated that he was fond of Kay but that she was very aggressive and that she ended the arrangement when he would not leave Ena to marry her. In that regard, he was probably as close to the truth as in anything he ever said about the murders.

In his confession, Harold detailed trysts at various motels and admitted he and Kay had sex on an average of at least once a week before Ena became involved. In the interview, though, Harold stated that he and Kay occasionally had sex at his house, that Ena was aware of it, and that on occasion she was there at the time but did not participate. Very few wives are so supremely indifferent that they would read a magazine or watch television while their husband was in the house with his mistress.

During the interview, Harold denied having poured weed killer on Kay's lawn after their relationship ended, and he also denied pouring sugar in the gas tank of her car and mailing her a lightbulb that had been painted red, all of which he had admitted to in his confession. In both the confession and the interview, he admitted to having painted some of the graffiti about Kay's sexual activities on bridges and signs in the area, but in both instances, he denied painting all of them.

As previously stated, Harold had not been contacted by law enforcement personnel during the graffiti investigation in the summer of 1973. McCook chief of police William Green had had W. W. Tumblin removed from the Ida Fitzgibbons investigation, and that may have soured Tumblin on digging deeply into any situation. Green then decided Fitzgibbons's death was a suicide. But that decision did not meet with general approbation and may well have meant Nokes did not fear investigation. And the patrol, in what certainly constituted negligence, paid for its action at the hands of the legislature.

On December 12 Capt. V. B. Byler of the patrol wrote to Starrett, apologizing for the delay in responding occasioned by the Hoyt murders and stating, "After exhaustive investigation and an extensive study of this case, I find myself in essentially the same position that you and Chief William Green have reached."

On December 19 Starrett wrote to Byler, saying he did not accept Green's determination of suicide by Fitzgibbons: "In that we have difficulties enough, I didn't want to make an issue of our differences as to the cause of her death. By the same token, I do not care to be untruthful and it was most inadvertent, if at any time I indicated that I thought the death of Ida G. Fitzgibbons to be a suicide."

In 1976 after a number of complaints by residents of Nebraska, including some from McCook, the Nebraska legislature passed Resolution 141, to investigate law enforcement in Nebraska, especially the Criminal Division of the state patrol. A select committee was created, consisting of Sen. John DeCamp as the chair, Sen. Doug Bereuter, Sen. Ernie Chambers, Sen. Don Dworak, Sen. Steve Fowler, Sen. Bill Nichol, Sen. Barry Reutzel, and Sen. Loran Schmit. Lincoln attorney Toney Redman was chosen as counsel.

One of the cases chosen for investigation was the Ida Fitzgibbons case. Committee counsel Redman grilled Lt. Donald Grieb as to what the patrol had done independently to investigate the Fitzgibbons case, other than to rely on Green's work. After the questioning, the committee concluded, "Looking through the information we have been able to obtain, we found no reports indicating that the Nebraska State Patrol reinvestigated those portions of the case already covered by Green to determine if his reports and accounting were accurate, particularly the allegations that the deceased was despondent."

Redman's colloquy to Grieb went like this:

Q. (Redman) Did you put a great deal of reliance on Green's investigation?

A. (Grieb) I did. I put a lot of reliance when I first talked to Chief Green and when I went out and I backed up a lot of things that he had said. I've always relied on what Chief Green has told me and from the information that bares [*sic*] out the facts most of the things that he told me, showed that he was right.

After holding several hearings, the committee issued its Ida G. Fitzgibbons report. It concluded, "The original investigation conducted under the authority of Chief Green appears to be totally inadequate, lacking in professionalism, and the entire conduct of Chief Green suggests that there may have been an intentional effort by Green, for whatever reason, to justify a suicide theory during the coroner's inquest at the expense of the facts."

Stung, Green sued the committee in U.S. district court in Lincoln. He alleged that the committee deprived him of a property interest, his reputation, without due process in violation of the Fourteenth Amendment to the U.S. Constitution. Green lost in the district court. He appealed. He lost again in the Eighth Circuit Court of Appeals. In an opinion (612 F2d 368) dated January 4, 1980, the Eighth Circuit held that a stigma to one's reputation was not a property or liberty interest protected by the Fourteenth Amendment.

The action of the patrol in accepting Green's finding of suicide virtually without investigation was clearly faulty. Whether the removal of Tumblin from the Fitzgibbons case was wrong is a more difficult question. But it is clear that Lieutenant Grieb made no real effort to placate Tumblin and that he and Tumblin remained at odds thereafter. If they had not been antagonistic, perhaps Tumblin would have been more diligent in his investigation of the sign painting in the late summer of 1973. He might have questioned Harold Nokes, when Kay Hein had acknowledged Nokes to have been a lover. If Nokes had known that law enforcement knew of his relationship with Kay, it might have put him on his guard and lessened his reliance on gun play. For want of a nail, the shoe was lost.

But as "Dandy" Don Meradith, the charming raconteur, frequently reminded his listeners on Monday Night Football, "if ifs and buts were candy and nuts, what a Merry Christmas we would have." The subpar performance of the state patrol on the graffiti investigation may well have been a link in the chain of causation that brought about the death of the Hoyts. But Harold Nokes, by his own admission, was the killer, and no one really knows why he acted as he did.

Why did Harold Nokes kill the Hoyts? Why did he harass Kay? How would he benefit by frightening and angering her? Would anything have warned Nokes that he should not be ruled by his passion? In an effort to learn what might have motivated Nokes, much of the relevant information discovered by the authorities and related by some of the parties was presented by the author in oral form in 2008 to Dr. John Baldwin, a forensic psychiatrist. Dr. Baldwin has been an expert witness in a number of criminal prosecutions, most notably that of Duane Earl Pope, tried in federal court in Nebraska for the murder of three bank employees in an abortive attempt to rob a bank in Big Springs, Nebraska, in 1965. Based solely on the information presented to him, Dr. Baldwin gave an opinion as best he could as to why the parties did what they claimed or admitted.

Dr. Baldwin felt that Harold Nokes was probably tired and bored with his wife. He was flattered by the attention of Kay Hein, and once he started receiving her sexual favors, he could not bear to stop. He became addicted. His reason fled.

Dr. Baldwin believes that Harold could not bear to believe

that Kay tired of the affair after she realized that marriage to Harold was not in the cards. Harold then transferred his anger at her onto her parents. Harold thought the parents were the problem, since they had chastised him about demanding blackmail money from Kay. Because he had been successful in enticing Kay and Ena into the ménage à trois, he believed he could convince the Hoyts that there was nothing amiss in their relationship with Kay. Kay had spurned him and turned to her parents for help, so the only way he could seek revenge was to pacify or eliminate the parents.

Dr. Baldwin speculated Nokes must have believed that if he could not persuade the Hoyts with logical arguments, he could intimidate them, which may have been his reason for taking the pistol along when visiting their home, if in fact he did take a gun. The ultimate act of shooting the Hoyts was a manifestation of Harold's belief that he had to win, no matter what, and a way to take revenge on Kay for her leaving him.

Dr. Baldwin thought it was highly unusual for Ena Nokes to have been involved in the sexual relationship and speculated that the Nokeses might have had a shared psychosis, a folie à deux, a mental disorder in which the personality is seriously disorganized.

Dr. Baldwin thought Kay might well have been bipolar, a personality disorder characterized by episodes of mania and depression. Kay's promiscuity, her lack of judgment, and her lack of restraint were symptomatic of the disorder.

Owen and Donna Elmer, Kay's sister and brother-in-law, graciously discussed in detail Kay's behavior during her childhood and adolescence and her relationship with her parents. The Elmers blamed Kay for the motives that led to the death of the Hoyts and felt that Kay's actions had driven a wedge between each of the five Hoyt siblings. Stanley and Herbert, the youngest two brothers, took Kay's side and felt Donna should have stepped in and stopped Kay's sexual relationship with the Nokeses, though the Elmers were unaware of it until after the death of the Hoyts. It is interesting to note that Roger (Whitey), the eldest child and now deceased, and Donna were the two siblings who had the best opportunity to observe Kay, her dealings with her parents, and her total modus operandi. They had learned of Mrs. Hoyt's concerns about Kay's actions. The two younger brothers were in the service, far removed from McCook.

The Elmers were fond of DeWayne Hein, Kay's former husband, and felt he was a fine man and a good father, an opinion they frequently communicated to Kay. The Elmers watched Kay's children when she was out of town, knowing she had gone to Kansas City with the Nokeses, although they did not know Harold or Ena. They did know Kay had received a black eye on that trip, an injury she refused to discuss.

The Elmers felt strongly that Mr. and Mrs. Hoyt would have been extremely unlikely to have voluntarily gone to McCook with the Nokeses or to have allowed Ena Nokes to drive their car, and they suspected there must have been some form of coercion involved.

Kay's possible complicity in the murders continues to trouble the Elmers. One fact never explained in the investigation and evaded by Kay was her engagement of a babysitter on the night of the murders, while she remained at home, waiting for a telephone call that never came. It would seem logical that with a sitter in place, Kay was planning to leave her home when the call came. Whom was she going to meet? Had Harold purchased her participation by telling her that he was willing to divorce Ena and marry her? Was she still so in love with Harold that she was willing to return to the threesome if there were parental approbation? Or was she simply waiting for a call from one of her more recent sexual partners?

What possible difference in the lives of Harold and Ena would a peace treaty with the Hoyts have made? Only if placating the Hoyts were necessary before Kay would be willing to resume the affair does it make any sense for Harold and Ena to have gone to the Hoyt farm on that fateful Sunday night. It makes no sense for Ena to have gone to the farm if Harold had agreed to divorce Ena and marry Kay. But if this were the case, perhaps Ena did not know. In any event, it seems that Harold felt it was necessary that Kay's parents be convinced he was a decent man. With the Hoyts farming near Culbertson and the Nokeses living in McCook, years might pass without the parties running into each other. And other than moral reproach, the Hoyts could not bring pressure to bear on the Nokeses. Other than to gain the Hoyts' approval of his character, there is no apparent reason for the Nokeses to have driven to the Hoyt farm.

There are some flaws in this theory. From all indications, Kay and Harold had had no meaningful conversations for some time prior to September 23. Kay must have suspected Harold was the perpetrator in painting the graffiti, ruining her yard, and pouring sugar in her gas tank. He had talked to her about her need for a red lightbulb. Indeed, she had fingered Harold as a possible culprit when she was interrogated by Tumblin and Deputy Haegen concerning the graffiti. Yet as late as mid-November, Bob Sawdon reported to Judge Jack Hendrix that he was sure Kay was not telling all she knew about the killings and added that he suspected she was still in love with Harold and was concealing evidence to protect him. Despite the bizarre relationship between Kay and the Nokeses, it is possible that they had reached some sort of détente by September 23 and that they were going to attempt to allay the fears and concerns that Edwin and Wilma Hoyt had concerning the relationship. Thus, the Elmers' fears about Kay's involvement may well be justified.

Sawdon's evaluation of Kay's cooperation and of her feelings for Harold is entitled to careful analysis. He was a persistent investigator. He and Lannie Roblee broke the case open—Sawdon by forcing Kay Hein to admit the sexual relationship, Roblee by impelling Harold Nokes to confess. Sawdon's assumption of the lead role in the investigation, after he had been hired by Fred Schroeder, bothered some of the state patrol investigators, who felt that Sawdon was self-aggrandizing. Nonetheless, the evidence that he turned up through his relentless questioning of Kay Hein was crucial to the case against the Nokeses.

It is quite interesting, therefore, that Sawdon was not present on January 4, 1974, when Harold Nokes's confession was transcribed by a court reporter. The statement was taken at Fred Schroeder's office in Curtis, but Schroeder was not in the room when the statement was taken. Paul Douglas and Lannie Roblee represented the state, and Dick Hove represented Harold Nokes. Why was Sawdon omitted?

Harold Nokes had told Roblee, in his oral confession, that the murders had taken place at his home in McCook. Thus the proper venue for all further legal proceedings would be in Red Willow County, but Clyde Starrett, the Red Willow County attorney, was not present at the formal confession either. His absence, however, has been explained earlier.

Paul Douglas, who questioned Harold Nokes, was a highly capable and experienced prosecutor. He obviously did not believe much of Harold's story, especially why Nokes took his gun to the Hoyt home and the manner in which he shot the Hoyts. But there was no need for rigorous cross-examination. The case had been solved. The murderer had confessed and faced either death or life in prison. Douglas had a voluntary confession that would stand up in court, given in the presence of Harold Nokes's attorney. Delving into the inconsistencies was not necessary, so a number of questions were left unresolved.

Why would the Hoyts agree to go to the Nokeses' home to discuss Kay? Were they coerced into going? If they were going to talk to Kay, why didn't they call her from their home to see if she was at home and willing, before agreeing to go to McCook with the Nokeses? Why were both willing to ride with Harold Nokes and to let Ena Nokes drive their car?

It is difficult to believe that the Hoyts were taken to McCook at gunpoint. There were two of them, and if Harold Nokes were driving them, he would have needed to keep his gun on at least one of them with his weakened right hand while he drove with his left. It is possible that Harold made Edwin Hoyt drive and Wilma sit beside him in back, while he covered them both with his gun. But if that were the case, why didn't Harold have them drive him in their car, while Ena drove the Nokeses' car?

Perhaps the Hoyts were already dead. Perhaps the murder occurred at their farm. But there were no traces of blood at the Hoyt farm or in the Nokeses' car. And why would the Nokeses take the bodies to McCook when they could have been dumped in a rural area? Perhaps Kay, at Harold's instigation, had already called her parents and asked them to come to the Nokeses' home, where they could all talk. Perhaps the call she was waiting for was to be from Harold, advising her that they had all reached the Nokeses' home. But if so, why didn't she call the Nokeses during the evening, to see if they had arrived?

Harold Nokes's account of how he handled his gun on the night of the murders does not ring true. He must have known it was dangerous to carry a loaded and cocked pistol.

He was very familiar with firearms. He must have known it was virtually impossible to release the safety with the thumb of his left hand if he was holding the gun in his left hand with his finger on the trigger. He also must have known that it was a real possibility that the sight on the top of the barrel would catch on his belt as he tried to draw the gun out of his trousers.

A more rational chronology leading up to the killing of Edwin Hoyt would begin with the argument between Hoyt and Harold Nokes as they exited the car at Nokes's home. The argument prompted Nokes to suggest they go to the basement so their voices would not be heard by the neighbors. Harold then turned on the light so Hoyt could see his way down the steps. While Hoyt descended to the basement, Nokes went to his bedroom and retrieved his gun from the dresser. He then went to the basement, where he confronted Hoyt. Hoyt may have attempted to wrest the gun away from Nokes, who shot him more than once, enough times that it was clear that Hoyt was dead. Pulling the gun from his belt, releasing the safety, and shooting Edwin Hoyt while Hoyt covered three feet—one stride—as Harold stated in his confession, defies considerations of time and space and digital flexibility.

While supervising the transcribing of Harold Nokes's confession, Douglas pointed out to Nokes that there was no need to kill Wilma Hoyt, if she were attempting to run upstairs. Nokes could have caught her and pulled her back. There is no physical evidence to establish that she tried to run. Rather, she may have been taken into the laundry room at gunpoint and eliminated as a witness. She may have been shot more than once or shot in the head. For Harold Nokes to have killed both of the Hoyts with one shot each, and in such short order, would have been very good marksmanship, especially with his left hand.

Why cut up the bodies? Why not drag them upstairs, put them in their car, drive it to Strunk Lake or Trenton Lake, and sink it? Even if Harold's right arm was as crippled as he maintained, Ena could have assisted him. Perhaps loading the bodies into a car would be observed by the neighbors. But this was late at night, and the neighbors might well have been asleep. No one reported any gunshots to the McCook police, even though Ena's reconnaissance after the shootings indicated neighbors were outside with their porch light on. No one mentioned Ena dragging the hose downstairs.

Perhaps Nokes felt that the bodies had to be dissected to conceal the number of bullet wounds in each corpse. But was he capable of dismembering them both by himself? Surely Ena did more than wrap remnants in freezer paper. While they were at this grisly task, why didn't the Nokeses cut off Mrs. Hoyt's fingers, with rings that surely could be identified? (Donna Elmer has stated that Mrs. Hoyt, who suffered from arthritis, had swollen and misshapen fingers and that the rings could not have been easily removed by simply pulling them over her fingers.)

Why did the Nokeses choose to dispose of the dismembered bodies in the lake? Harold disposed of the viscera by dumping it in a remote canyon, where it was likely eaten by scavenging animals. Few people venture into the rugged canyons west of McCook except on very specific errands. Bodies in those canyons could remain undiscovered for weeks. Harold Nokes was familiar with the inaccessible terrain. Although it might have taken an evening or two, the body parts could have been similarly hidden.

Taking the frozen body parts to Strunk Lake posed a number of problems for Harold Nokes. Neighbors noticed and wondered why he was taking his boat out in the dark on an early fall rainy evening. Did the neighbors wonder why Harold was going boating if his father was so ill that he might have to leave at any hour of the night as he had told the Walkers? As an outdoorsman and boater, Harold must have realized that there was a risk that some of the body parts might surface, as indeed they did. Was the lake a better disposal ground than a remote and inaccessible canyon?

The role Ena Nokes played in the killings and their aftermath was by no means minor. According to Harold, she drove the Hoyt car to McCook, then parked it at the hospital after the murders. Even taking his defense of her at face value, she wrapped the body parts in freezer paper, bought plastic trash cans for storage of the body parts, and accompanied him to the disposal area at Strunk Lake. She washed the Nokeses' basement to remove all traces of blood, flesh, and viscera. She was, by any recognized legal theory, an abettor in both murders and in their concealment. Why was she not so charged?

Harold's motivation for the protection of Ena has been discussed previously. But why were the authorities willing to make a deal with him? He had very little bargaining power. He had already orally confessed to Lannie Roblee before any plea bargaining commenced. Roblee could have established the crime in testimony even if no written statement was taken. In both his oral statement and in his written confession, Harold furnished the details of Ena's involvement in the case. Apparently the prosecution felt that since Harold was clearly the killer, lighter treatment for Ena could be justified. Perhaps Paul Douglas, who had plenty on his plate in Lincoln, felt that having to prepare and prosecute a tedious yet sensational trial in McCook was not worth the effort, if Harold would plead guilty once Ena was charged with a much lesser offense. In addition, he had no evidence that Ena had killed either of the Hoyts.

Indeed, Douglas has acknowledged that Harold Nokes's

confession was sufficient to put him away, while trying Ena would be both expensive and time consuming. Frontier County had little money, and although Red Willow County would ultimately be responsible for the costs, that county was not at all enthusiastic about investigating and prosecuting the crimes. Lannie Roblee has stated that Frontier County ultimately billed Red Willow County for all its costs incurred in the case, and Red Willow County refused to pay.

Looking at the crime in retrospect, certain details can be taken as facts. Harold Nokes and Ena Nokes and Kay Hein engaged in a sexual triangle. Edwin and Wilma Hoyt were shot and killed. Harold Nokes confessed to the crime, although it is conceivable that Ena, familiar with guns, might have shot one or both. The dismembered bodies were thrown in Harry Strunk Lake. Some body parts ultimately surfaced. Beyond these facts, virtually everything about the murders remains unresolved. And since none of the three principal players is willing to talk about what really transpired, one can only speculate as to the who, what, when, where, and why of the events.

The most plausible reason for the Hoyts to have gone to McCook on the fatal evening is that they did so under coercion. Harold Nokes may have displayed the gun at their home and threatened to shoot. The Hoyts could have feared trying to wrest the gun from him on the trip to McCook. The threat of the gun may have been why Ena drove the Hoyt car to McCook. Or perhaps the Nokeses never went to the Hoyt farm and simply intercepted them at the hospital as they responded to a spurious emergency call from Kay. But if so, why did the position of their car seat indicate that it was last driven by a short person?

If Harold Nokes had shot each of the Hoyts more than once, it would have indicated a murderous intent, thus necessitating the dissection of the bodies. But why didn't he simply take the Hoyts to Massacre Canyon and shoot them there? There must have been some agreement with Kay that they would be brought to McCook. Thus the need for her babysitter, and thus the need to take the Hoyts to the Nokeses' home.

Another troubling aspect of the case is that so little real evidence was gathered as the result of bugging the Nokeses' home. A master tape was kept running all the time for almost three weeks, yet the only really incriminating evidence was Harold's comment that "we should have removed the rings," a comment that was unsolicited and evoked no response. The bugs were not installed until early December, so it may be that the Nokeses had talked the matter over ad nauseam by then and had no need to discuss it further. They did talk about committing suicide if they were charged with murder and discussed the implementation of suicide. The bug yielded no details of the crime in the time that it was in operation.

In her testimony before Judge Hendrix on the application to bug the Nokeses' house, Kay Hein may have lied about the fact that she had nothing further to do with the Nokeses after the affair ended. It may well have been part of a macabre plot against her parents. Her evasiveness when questioned by the patrol as to why she hired a babysitter on the night of the killings, but never left home, certainly raises unanswered questions as to her part, if any, in the transportation of her parents to McCook.

Society imposed jail sentences on both Harold and Ena Nokes. If Kay was complicit, she escaped punishment.

8

The Postlude

Murder affects innumerable lives. It ends those of the victim or victims and wreaks havoc on their families and friends. It may terminate the freedom of the killers and cause society in general to reflect on the sanctity of lives and the fairness and efficiency of the judicial system. The murders of Edwin and Wilma Hoyt are a graphic case in point.

Both of the Hoyts were literally cut down in the prime of their lives. But even more poignant is the fact that their murders, growing as they did out of the actions of one of their children, created a substantial rift among their offspring, a division that still exists today, forty years later. Even extended members of the Hoyt family willing to respond to inquiries about the impact of the killings on the family refuse to be identified as informants, for fear of exacerbating the breach. Only Owen and Donna Elmer, targets of some of the rancor, and Jerry Ann Hoyt, widow of the Hoyts' eldest son, "Whitey," are willing to speak for attribution about the impact of the slayings.

The passage of time has lessened the impact of the murders in McCook. A new generation has no knowledge of either the Hoyts or the Nokeses. Conversations on the streets of the city are more concerned with economic development and the lack of water in the Republican River than in evaluating the action of the Nokeses.

But there are still those in McCook, and even across

Nebraska, who remember the killings and the gruesome dumping of the bodies. Few murders in Nebraska in the ensuing years have involved such brutal treatment of the bodies of the victims. One, occurring in far western Nebraska, involved the killing by Raymond Mata of the small child of his paramour. He cut up the body of the child, fed some of it to his dog, and flushed portions of it down his toilet. His savagery earned him a spot on Nebraska's death row.

Today, Harold Nokes might well have received the death penalty for his crime. The Supreme Court of the United States has recently held that the presence or absence of aggravating circumstances in capital cases must be determined by a jury, rather than by a judicial panel. And a jury whose conscience was shocked by the awful dismemberment of the bodies of the Hoyts might well nullify any judicial instructions to the contrary and find that aggravating circumstances were present, even though the dismemberment took place after death.

Of course, Harold Nokes pleaded guilty, and no jury heard evidence of the ménage à trois that led to the death of the Hoyts. Were the case to be heard today, even on a guilty plea, a jury in the first-degree murder case of Wilma Hoyt would have to hear aggravating circumstances and might well learn of the existence of the sexual threesome that started the participants down the path to perdition. Even with today's relaxed moral code, Red Willow County jurors might find that a killing growing out of aberrant sex that was carried out to conceal a crime was an extremely aggravating circumstance.

After a lengthy effort to find Ena Nokes, I received information about her place of residence. Accompanied by retired district judge Samuel Van Pelt, I went to her apartment in Lincoln near the East Campus of the University of Nebraska. The building is restricted to occupancy by low-income seniors. She responded to a knock but refused admission to her apartment. She acknowledged she knew who I was and that I was preparing a book about the case. I informed her that the book would present a different story than that told at the time of the murders; she refused an offer to tell her side of the story and closed the door.

It has proven difficult to track Ena Nokes's activity after she was paroled from prison. She moved to Lincoln and has held positions in business offices as well as operating a service sharpening shears and other implements. She is eighty-four years old and seems to be retired. Her hair is snow white, but she appears to be in good health. The Nokeses' son, Leslie Allen Nokes, farms near Minden, Nebraska, and Ena frequently attends church in Minden with him.

Finding Kay Hein proved difficult as well. To all intents and purposes, for many years Kay Hein disappeared from McCook and even Nebraska, her whereabouts unknown to most. When she left McCook, she severed all her connections with her local family and her past. The Elmers related that before Harold was sentenced, a friend of Kay's drove her and her girls to Kansas, where they caught a bus to Denver and a train to California. Kay has never returned to McCook. She went to work at Castle Air Force Base, near the home of her uncle, Thurber Hoyt. She married a man named James Allen, and for some time the Allens operated a fruit business in Merced, California. They then decided to move to Harpster, Idaho, where James subsequently died. Kay was in Harpster during the period of time I tried to contact her, from 2005 to 2010.

Jerry Anne Hoyt saved a letter written by Kay to Whitey and his family after Kay left McCook. The letter, which was a shock and a surprise to Whitey and Jerry Anne, is dated April 7, 1974, though the Hoyts did not receive it until much later. Kay wrote that she had found God. The letter attempted to explain Kay's motive in gifts from her parents. She said that she kept the gifts only because they arrived at her house when she was gone. She told Whitey that if he felt she should not have received the gifts—a washer and a television set—they could deduct their cost from her share of their parents' estate.

She discussed the possible sale of her house, which took place on April 29, 1974, and talked of her difficult financial situation. She said she had a job at Castle Air Force Base, a job that may have been aided by the air force position of Thurber Hoyt. The letter gives no explanation of her relationship with the Nokeses other than her mention that she was involved with a married man who would not marry her. Kay does not offer an apology for any role she may have had in her parents' death and gave no reason for her sudden departure from McCook. Why the letter was sent and what Kay hoped to achieve by sending it puzzled Whitey and Jerry Anne.

Jerry Anne Hoyt recalled that Whitey wanted nothing to do with Kay after the deaths of their parents and, on one occasion, while visiting Thurber Hoyt in Merced, said he would leave if Thurber called Kay to come see him. Her letter worked no magic in healing a rift with Whitey.

Jerry Anne Hoyt received a phone call from Kay in 2008 at her quilt shop in Kansas. Jerry Anne was busy with customers at the time, and the call was somewhat disjointed as a consequence. Kay gave no reason for having been out of touch for so long but told Jerry Anne she was living in Idaho. She told her of the whereabouts of her girls, furnished her phone number, and asked several questions about quilting, telling Jerry Anne that she now had a quilting machine. Jerry Anne was flabbergasted to have received the call, had no idea how Kay got the phone number of her store, and has not heard from Kay since.

If Kay were truly distressed by the murder of her parents, it seems only reasonable that she would have wanted to remain in McCook to see justice done, to see punishment meted out to Harold Nokes for his acts against her and her parents. But severing all family ties, she left McCook at night, without warning or notice. Was she afraid that Harold might incriminate her at his sentencing?

The Elmers report that after Kay moved to California, she had difficulty with both of her daughters. One ran away from home in the company of a young man who later jilted her. DeWayne Hein, who had tried to gain custody of both girls after their move to California and who had been deterred from doing so because of the expense, discovered where his daughter had gone, went after her, and brought her back to his home in Yuma, Colorado.

Kay did not respond to my letters asking if she desired to tell her side of the story for the book. I had her social security number, and a lawyer friend skilled in tracking impecunious debtors was able to discover her address and phone number. An early morning phone call to her residence caught her by surprise. She refused to acknowledge that she was Kay Hein, saying that Kay was not present at the time but that she would give her a message. Upon being informed about the book, she responded that Kay Hein would not want to talk about the case anyway and hung up. The Elmers stated that Kay called one of her brothers and told him of the call and the proposed book. The brother's wife then called the Elmers and passed the information along.

After Kay was widowed and while still in Harpster, she contacted a former high school classmate, Vince Wasia, who lived in California and whose wife had died. She and Wasia, who was the biggest star in the backfield of the all-conquering 1960 McCook High football team, have since married, and they now live in New Braunfels, Texas. They attended a McCook High School reunion held in Goodyear, Arizona, in 2011. Those in attendance did not discuss the murders with her. Apparently she no longer fears discovery of her whereabouts.

None of the participants want to talk about the case. Advancing age seems to have reconciled them to their fate. Harold is eighty-five, Ena eighty-four, Kay seventy. Perhaps they cannot remember what transpired. Perhaps, as Harold did in his interview, they have conjured up in their own minds a version of the story they can live with, a story that does not trouble their conscience every waking hour. But it is unlikely that they do not think of the murders at all.

Those familiar with the case, those whose lives have been affected as much as the lives of the three participants, have obviously thought about what has transpired and what might have happened. What if Harold had divorced Ena and married Kay? What if Kay, instead of turning to other sexual outlets for consolation, had left McCook to start a new life elsewhere? What if Harold's pistol had misfired or if he had given Edwin Hoyt warning that he had a gun?

After such speculation, the question remains, why did Harold and Ena Nokes murder Edwin and Wilma Hoyt? What purpose did the killings serve? Most people would find it difficult to imagine a sexual passion so fervent that the passionate would kill to maintain it. And it is even more difficult to understand why Harold thought that killing Kay's parents would bring a frightened Kay Hein back into the affair. Perhaps the theory advanced by Dr. Baldwin is the answer—Harold Nokes felt he had to win at all costs.

Those who support the death penalty may feel that Harold Nokes was not punished as severely as he deserved. The death and dismemberment of two innocent people, especially if it

were to coerce Kay Hein into returning to the sexual relationship, has to be considered especially heinous. But Harold
Nokes has lost his freedom. He has spent thirty-nine years
in prison. He knows he will die there. Even if the punishment
does not fit the crime, it is a severe and continuing depriva-
tion of liberty.

The party least impacted by the crime is Ena Nokes. Even
though she lost her husband, to all intents and purposes, and
spent two years in prison, she was more culpable than she
appeared. She stated to Kay Hein that her fear of losing Harold
was her justification for embarking on the affair. But once Kay
Hein terminated the relationship, why was she not content?
Why not tell Harold, "Kay is gone. Let's resume our normal
marital relationship"? Instead, she told Kay how much the
relationship meant to her. She tried as diligently as Harold
to bring Kay back into the fold. She went to the Hoyt home
with Harold. She assisted in dissecting the bodies. She helped
take them to the lake. It is no wonder that she is not anxious
to discuss what took place or her role in all of it.

Ena sees Harold regularly. Harold told me in 2007 that
she visits him twice a week. What do they have in common
now? What can they discuss? There is no statute of limitations
for murder, and she may well fear a death bed confession
on his part.

Kay Hein must be consumed by remorse. She no longer
has familial roots in Nebraska, where she has been ostra-
cized by the family members remaining there. She has to
bear the burden of knowing that her illicit sexual activity, her
attempt to win over another woman's husband and to destroy
a marriage, led directly to the murder of her parents and the
figurative destruction of her extended family.

If the parties had acted rationally and moved forward to
pick up the pieces of their lives and soldiered on after the

sexual relationship had terminated, things would have been very, very different. But they did not. And it is that irrationality that makes this such a compelling story today. As Whittier said many years ago, "Of all sad words of tongue or pen, the saddest are these—'It might have been.'"

Slipping Backward: A History of
the Nebraska Supreme Court
James W. Hewitt

Law and Order in Buffalo Bill's Country:
Legal Culture and Community on
the Great Plains, 1867–1910
Mark R. Ellis

The Nebraska-Kansas Act of 1854
John R. Wunder and Joann M. Ross

Women Who Kill Men: California
Courts, Gender, and the Press
Gordon Morris Bakken and
Brenda Farrington

Called to Justice: The Life of
a Federal Trial Judge
Warren K. Urbom

Sunflower Justice: A New History
of the Kansas Supreme Court
R. Alton Lee

In Cold Storage: Sex and Murder on the Plains
James W. Hewitt

To order or obtain more information on
these or other University of Nebraska Press
titles, visit www.nebraskapress.unl.edu.

CPSIA information can be obtained
at www.ICGtesting.com
Printed in the USA
LVHW031139160721
692882LV00006B/354

9 780803 256637